M000103633

THE DOCTORS OF THE CHURCH
Volume Two

BY THE SAME AUTHOR

Moments in Catholic History

Traveling with Jesus in the Holy Land

Married Saints

The Mission and Future of the Catholic Press (Editor)

Visit our website at
WWW.ALBAHOUSE.ORG

The Doctors of the Church

*An Introduction to
the Church's Great Teachers*

VOLUME TWO:
DOCTORS OF THE SECOND MILLENNIUM

JOHN F. FINK

ALBA·HOUSE　　NEW·YORK
SOCIETY OF ST. PAUL, 2187 VICTORY BLVD., STATEN ISLAND, NEW YORK 10314

ST PAULS

Library of Congress Cataloging-in-Publication Data

Fink, John F.
    The doctors of the Church : an introduction to the Church's
great teachers / John F. Fink.
        p. cm.
    Contents: v. 1. Doctors of the first millennium — v. 2. Doctors
of the second millennium.
    ISBN 0-8189-0841-6 (set) — ISBN 0-8189-0839-4 (v. 1) —
ISBN 0-8189-0840-8 (v. 2)
    1. Doctors of the church—Biography. 2. Doctors of the
church. I. Title.

    BX4669.F56 2000
    282—dc21   99-28459

Produced and designed in the United States of America by the
Fathers and Brothers of the Society of St. Paul,
2187 Victory Boulevard, Staten Island, New York 10314-6603,
as part of their communications apostolate.

ISBN: 0-8189-0839-4 Doctors of the Church, Volume 1
ISBN: 0-8189-0840-8 Doctors of the Church, Volume 2
ISBN: 0-8189-0841-6 Doctors of the Church, 2 Volume Set

Printing Information:

Current Printing - first digit   1   2   3   4   5   6   7   8   9   10

Year of Current Printing - first year shown

2000   2001   2002   2003   2004   2005   2006   2007   2008

DEDICATION

To Marie and Our Children:

Regina
Barbara
Robert
Stephen
Therese
David
John

TABLE OF CONTENTS

INTRODUCTION

No, this isn't a book about the great healers in the history of the Catholic Church. Although we sometimes seem to think of doctors as physicians, or perhaps dentists, the word "doctor" actually comes from the Latin *docere*, which means to teach. Historically, as those in academic communities know, "doctor" has been the title of an accomplished teacher. Today a doctorate remains the highest academic degree in a particular field.

In the Catholic Church, the title "Doctor of the Church" has been given to a relatively small number of men and women — thirty-three, to be exact — whose combination of intellectual brilliance and sanctity has been of extraordinary importance in the development of doctrine or spirituality. All of them have made lasting contributions to the understanding of the Catholic faith and are recognized for their great merits. However, the title does not necessarily infer that everything they wrote is free of errors.

The Church has recognized three categories of outstanding Christian writers: the Apostolic Fathers, the Fathers of the Church, and the Doctors of the Church. The Apostolic Fathers were Christian writers of the first and second centuries whose writings were derived from Christ's Apostles. Chief among them are Saint Clement, the third successor of Saint Peter as bishop of Rome; Saint Ignatius of Antioch, the second successor of Saint Peter in that see and a disciple of Saint John the Apostle; and Saint Polycarp, bishop of Smyrna and another disciple of Saint John. The unknown authors of the *Didache*, an important record of Christian belief, practice and governance from the second century, are also considered to be Apostolic Fathers.

The Fathers of the Church were theologians and writers of the first eight centuries who were known for their learning and holiness. Some were popes while others were lawyers, theologians, monks or hermits. Depending upon what list you consult, there were about a hundred Fathers of the Church, usually divided between Greek Fathers and Latin Fathers. This division was not only by language but by whether they lived in the Eastern or Western worlds. They also were sometimes divided between Ante-Nicene Fathers, who lived before the Council of Nicaea in 325; the Nicene Fathers who guided the Church during the fourth century when so much doctrine was formulated; and Post-Nicene Fathers, who lived after the fourth century.

Obviously, not all one hundred or so of these Fathers of the Church were equal in their learning or influence on the Church. Therefore, the greatest of the Fathers were also considered to be the Doctors of the Church. Initially, the Doctors were considered to be Saints Augustine, Ambrose, Jerome, and Pope Gregory I (the Great). However, they were all from the West, so later four men from the East were added: Saints Athanasius, Basil, Gregory Nazianzen, and John Chrysostom. All of them lived between 297 (the date of Athanasius's birth) and 604 (when Gregory the Great died).

These eight men, then, were commonly recognized as the Doctors of the Church at least from the eighth century until the sixteenth century. Then, in 1567, Pope Pius V (now Saint Pius V) wanted to honor Saint Thomas Aquinas in a special way and he added him to the list of Doctors. Saint Bonaventure was added in 1588. The list remained at ten until the 1720's. Saint Anselm was added in 1720, Saint Isidore of Seville in 1722, and Saint Peter Chrysologus in 1729. Saint Leo the Great was added in 1754.

More than half of the Doctors were named during the nineteenth and twentieth centuries — nine in the nineteenth century and ten in the twentieth. Those honored in the 1800's were Saints Peter Damian, 1828; Bernard of Clairvaux, 1830; Francis de Sales, 1877; Cyril of Alexandria and Cyril of Jerusalem, both in 1882; John Damascene, 1890;

and Bede, 1899. Those named during the twentieth century were Saints Ephrem of Syria, 1920; Peter Canisius, 1925; John of the Cross, 1926; Robert Bellarmine and Albert the Great, both in 1931; Anthony of Padua, 1946; Lawrence of Brindisi, 1959; Teresa of Avila and Catherine of Siena, both in 1970; and Thérèse of Lisieux, 1997.

The list was an all-male club until 1970 and even today, although the last three named to the list were women, men Doctors outnumber women Doctors thirty to three.

Some of the Doctors have been honored with special titles. Saint Augustine is known as *Doctor Gratiae*, Doctor of Grace, because of the importance of his writings about the theology of grace. Saint Thomas Aquinas is known as both *Doctor Angelicus*, the Angelic Doctor, and *Doctor Communis*, the Common Doctor, the latter to denote his universality and timeliness to all who study the Church's teachings. Saint Anselm earned the title of *Doctor Marianus*, the Marian Doctor, through his writings about the Blessed Virgin Mary and her role in salvation history. Saint Bernard of Clairvaux is known as *Doctor Mellifluus*, the Mellifluous Doctor, because of his sweet but powerful preaching. Saint Bonaventure is referred to as *Doctor Seraphicus*, the Seraphic Doctor, because he was a Franciscan and Saint Francis once had a vision in which the crucified Christ was borne aloft by Seraphim. Finally, Saint Albert the Great is known as *Doctor Universalis*, the Universal Doctor, because of the vast extent of his theological and philosophical work.

In the chapters that follow, I will give profiles of each of the thirty-three Doctors of the Church. Each profile will be followed by one or more writings from that particular Doctor. Needless to say, the profiles cannot be full biographies and the writings can be little more than samples since this book is intended to be only a popular introduction to the Doctors of the Church. As one would expect, the writings of most of the Doctors are voluminous. I tried to choose excerpts that are representative of that particular Doctor's writings, but I also tried to choose works that would give an overall effect of providing a fairly thorough overview of Christian doctrine and practice through the centuries.

I chose to write about them in roughly chronological, rather than alphabetical order, in order to place them in their historical context and because some of the Doctors worked with, or were influenced by, other Doctors of the same era.

I hope, of course, that readers will want to read more of the writings of these Doctors of the Church and will avail themselves of opportunities to do so.

FOREWORD
TO VOLUME TWO

Sixteen of the thirty-three men and women who have been declared Doctors of the Church lived during the second Christian millennium, which, for the purposes of this work, began at the start of the eleventh century.

It was easy to divide this work into two volumes because there was a lapse of more than three hundred years between the last Doctor of the first millennium, Saint John Damascene, who died in 749, and the first Doctor of the second millennium, Saint Peter Damian, who died in 1072. As explained in the chapter about Saint Peter Damian, the period between those two Doctors was one of the darkest periods in the Church's history.

There are differences between the type of men and women declared Doctors of the Church during the first millennium and those selected in the second millennium. For one thing, eight of the Doctors of the first millennium were part of the Eastern Church, the area of the world where Christianity began. By contrast, all of the Doctors of the second millennium were from Europe. As Rome became the acknowledged center of the Catholic Church, the Church became westernized. This was hurried along by the break between the Eastern and Western Churches, officially dated from 1054, at the beginning of the second millennium. Although there have been attempts to reunite the Churches, especially by the Second Council of Lyons in 1274 and the Council of Florence in 1431-45, the efforts have never been successful. Meanwhile, although there have been canonized saints in the Americas, Africa and Asia, none of them has displayed the intellectual acumen required to be recognized as a Doctor of the Church.

The Doctors of the two millennia differed also in that the Church's doctrines were more defined in the last thousand years than they were in the first thousand. For one thing, this meant that the later teachers spent more time and energy explaining doctrine than in developing it. For another thing, the Doctors of the second millennium had the advantage of being able to quote from the writings of the Doctors of the first millennium — which some of them did with great frequency.

It probably is no coincidence that Doctors of the Church have appeared when the Church most needed them. That certainly was true during the fourth and fifth centuries, when thirteen of the Doctors lived and taught, because this was when the Church was combating the worst heresies about the person of Jesus. Great teachers arose again in the eleventh century when the Church was badly in need of reform, and in the sixteenth century after the Protestant Reformation, another dark period for the Church. Six of the sixteen Doctors in this volume lived in the sixteenth century.

It was probably the thirteenth century, though, that produced the real giants among the Doctors of the Church: Saints Anthony of Padua, Albert the Great, Thomas Aquinas, and Bonaventure.

The second millennium also produced three absolutely remarkable women: Saints Catherine of Siena, Teresa of Avila, and Thérèse of Lisieux. Undoubtedly there have always been great women saints in the Catholic Church, but these three stand out, two of them because they were able to accomplish so much in a male-dominated society, and the other because she was able to show everyone how to reach perfection through her "little way" of doing all the everyday things well. It took, though, until 1970 for any woman to be declared a Doctor of the Church.

No one knows which great theologians might be named Doctors in the future. A saint that I personally believe has been overlooked is Saint Thomas More. I believe that his religious writings and his defense of the Church were sufficient for him to be so recognized. It also seems to me almost a certainty that, if John Henry Newman is ever canonized, he will also be named a Doctor of the Church. Edith Stein would be a good candidate among the women.

BIBLIOGRAPHY AND
ACKNOWLEDGMENTS

It would be impossible to list all the many lives of saints that include biographies of some, or all, of the Doctors of the Church. I will, therefore, simply list those that I consulted during the writing of this volume:

I always read over the biography of the Doctor I was going to write about in *Butler's Lives of the Saints*, which was originally published in 1756-9, revised in 1926-38, and subsequent editions published in 1956, 1966, 1981 and 1982. HarperCollins published the edition I used in 1991.

Also helpful was a two-volume *Lives of Saints* published in 1953 and 1963 by John J. Crawley & Co. The company is no longer in existence and the books are out of print. Not all of the Doctors of the Church are in them, but some are. I also consulted *Saint of the Day*, a popular book published by St. Anthony Messenger Press. In addition, *The Oxford Dictionary of Popes*, published by Oxford University Press, was helpful for background information about some of the Doctors who had close ties with the papacy.

I also checked facts in three books published by Our Sunday Visitor Press: *Catholic Almanac*, *Encyclopedia of Saints*, and *Encyclopedia of Catholic History*. And to check historical facts, I used *The Oxford Illustrated History of Christianity*, published by Oxford University Press. I also found *An Outline History of the Church by Centuries*, published by B. Herder Book Co. way back in 1943, still valuable today.

Alba House has some excellent books about several of the Doctors. One of Lavinia Byrne's "Saints Alive Series" is *The Life and Wisdom of Catherine of Siena* and the book *John and Thérèse: Flames of Love* is about the influence of Saint John of the Cross in the life and writings of Saint Thérèse of Lisieux. Another book that was helpful in the profile about Saint Thérèse was *Maurice & Thérèse*, by Bishop Patrick Ahern, Auxiliary Bishop of New York, published by Doubleday. For the profile of Saint Thomas Aquinas I consulted, besides books already mentioned, *The Angelic Doctor: The Life and World of St. Thomas Aquinas*, by Matthew Bunson, published by Our Sunday Visitor.

Not surprising, Liguori Press has a number of books by and about Saint Alphonsus Liguori. I found *Never Stop Walking: The Life and Spirit of Saint Alphonsus Liguori*, by Nancy Fearon, IHM, particularly helpful.

The excerpts from the Doctors of the Church are, of course, from their writings. I should note that I kept the Scripture quotations in those excerpts as they were already quoted rather than use any of the modern translations.

For readers who would like to read more by the Doctors, I suggest they check their libraries and Catholic bookstores. Some of the writings are more available than others, especially those by Saints Thomas Aquinas, Bernard of Clairvaux, Catherine of Siena, Teresa of Avila, John of the Cross, Francis de Sales, Alphonsus Liguori, and Thérèse of Lisieux. One extremely valuable place to read more from the Doctors, as well as writings from other saints, is the Office of Readings, part of the Liturgy of the Hours that all Catholics are encouraged to pray.

THE DOCTORS OF THE CHURCH
Volume Two

CHAPTER 18

SAINT PETER DAMIAN

None of the Doctors of the Church lived in the ninth and tenth centuries. It was a period that some historians have called the darkest age for the Church. The State, whether Italy or Germany, controlled Church affairs. This control began with Charlemagne in the ninth century and reverted to powerful Roman families in the tenth century. Church officials couldn't even elect the pope. Until 962 one or another Roman family chose the pope, usually a member of that family. After that time the popes were usually selected by the German emperor. The popes were secular men, usually more intent on furthering their families' finances than caring for the Church.

It was the age of feudalism. One of the features of the feudal system was the right of the lord to appoint ecclesiastical offices, a practice that quickly resulted in simony — the buying and selling of Church positions. The clerical vocation became a quick route to wealth and power and, once in power, prelates often oppressed the poor. Clerical marriage and concubinage were prevalent and in some places the episcopacy itself became a hereditary position filled by a bishop's son.

Religious practices among the laity declined as corruption among the clergy grew. The preaching of sermons was largely discontinued, sacraments were neglected, attendance at Mass declined, superstition increased, and divorce was common. The need for reform was acute indeed.

That was the situation when Peter Damian was born at Ravenna, Italy in 1007. He was seven years old when an important synod was held in Ravenna. King Henry II of Germany (later Saint Henry) had just intervened to help Pope Benedict VIII defeat a rival for the papacy and both the emperor and the pope were intent on reforming the Church. The synod legislated against simony, among other things. It was the beginning of the attempts made during the eleventh century to reform the Church, attempts in which Peter Damian would play a prominent role.

Peter's parents both died when he was a child and he was put in the care of an older brother. The brother treated him more like a slave than a member of the family, making him a swineherd as soon as he was old enough. Another brother, though, who happened to be archpriest of Ravenna, took pity on Peter and, recognizing his intelligence, arranged for his education by sending him to good schools. It seems that the archpriest's name was Damian and Peter added that name to his own in thanksgiving for his brother's charity toward him.

Already at an early age, Peter demonstrated an unusual piety, an austerity that he continued throughout his life. He wore a hair shirt under his clothes, spent many hours in prayer, and fasted rigorously. He sought out poor people to eat with and liked to minister personally to their needs.

His education complete, he became a professor. But in 1035 he left his teaching position and joined the Benedictines of the reform of Saint Romuald at Fonte Avellana. Saint Romuald, who had died only eight years earlier, had united the monastic and hermit life, and this appealed to Peter. The monks lived two to a cell and occupied their days in prayer, fasting and reading. Peter adapted to this life eagerly, slept so little that he developed severe insomnia, and studied the Bible until he was well versed in Scripture.

Peter was so well admired by the other monks that they unanimously recommended that he become abbot upon the superior's death. Peter was reluctant to assume that position, though, so the abbot made it a matter of obedience. Therefore, when the abbot died in 1043, Peter succeeded him and proved to be a well-loved superior. He founded five other hermitages, appointing priors for them while they remained under his general direction. His emphasis was the need for reform in the Church and he made sure that his monks were part of that reform.

However, that reform had to start with the papacy. Pope Benedict VIII and Saint Henry had both died in 1024 and the pope was succeeded by his brother, John XIX. He died in 1032 and was succeeded by Pope Benedict IX, a notoriously wicked man. He was pope when Peter Damian became abbot. One of Peter's friends was the archpriest John Gratian. In 1045, in order to rid the Church of the wicked Pope Benedict IX, John Gratian offered him a large sum of money if he would abdicate. He did, and John Gratian became Pope Gregory VI. But Benedict soon regretted his decision and tried to depose Gregory. About the same time, another man, Sylvester, tried to assume the papacy. So there were three men vying for the papacy.

Gregory VI sought the aid of Emperor Henry III, who went to Italy and summoned a council to decide the matter. He accepted the resignations or forced abdications of all three men and selected a German bishop to be pope, reigning as Clement II. Clement began his own program of Church reform, but he died after a reign of only eight months and his successor, Pope Damasus II, died after only twenty-three days in office. So it wasn't until Pope Leo IX was selected by Emperor Henry III in 1049 that things started to settle down. He signaled that Church reform was about to begin in earnest when he appointed the Benedictine monk Hildebrand as one of his chief assistants. Hildebrand was to serve as a close adviser to five popes before being elected pope himself in 1073, taking the name Pope Gregory VII. He has gone down in history as one of the Church's greatest popes.

Meanwhile, Peter Damian continued to govern his hermitages. He did not know that Pope Benedict IX had been bribed to abdicate. In fact, in his letter of congratulations to Pope Gregory VI, he wrote that his election had struck a blow at simony. He later wrote another letter to Pope Clement II — the pope whose reign was only eight months — expressing disappointment at the slow pace of his reforms. Along with Hildebrand, he became one of the principal advisers to Pope Leo IX, who began to depose bishops who bought their offices, and he served the next pope, Victor II, similarly.

In 1051, Peter wrote the book *Liber Gomorrhianus*, dedicating it to Pope Leo IX. It attacked the many vices then prominent among the clergy, especially clerical marriage. Two years later, he wrote *Liber Gratissimus*, a defense of the legitimacy of ordinations even when the man paid money to obtain his office. He also wrote many letters, some one hundred seventy of which still exist. We also have fifty-three of his sermons and seven biographies, including one of St. Romuald. (An excerpt is quoted later in this chapter.) It was for all of these writings that he was declared a Doctor of the Church.

In 1057 Pope Stephen IX forced Peter to become the cardinal-bishop of Ostia. When Peter tried to refuse, the pope actually threatened him with excommunication! Once installed in Ostia, Peter immediately established a program of reform in his diocese, wiping out any form of simony and encouraging his priests to observe celibacy. He tried to get his diocesan clergy to live together and to have regular prayer schedules as if in a monastery, as Saint Augustine had done. He encouraged his priests to practice discipline, to avoid too comfortable living and needless travel. At one point he even wrote to the bishop of Besançon complaining that the priests there sat down when they were singing the psalms in the Divine Office. He tried to restore a Church of an earlier period during a time of much-needed reform.

As he grew older, Peter kept trying to resign as cardinal-bishop of Ostia, a request Pope Nicholas II, who succeeded Pope Stephen IX, always refused. Peter renewed his request to the next pope, Alexander II, who gave his consent out of respect for all Peter had done in his service to the Church and the papacy, reserving the right to call upon him from time to time. So Peter returned to his monastery as a simple monk, hoping to live out his life in prayer and writing.

Pope Alexander did indeed call upon Peter

from time to time. Once he sent Peter to Germany to pass judgment on the request of the young king, Henry IV, for a divorce from his wife Bertha. Peter decided in favor of Bertha. Another time the pope sent Peter to Ravenna to settle troubles there after the archbishop had been excommunicated. When Peter arrived he found that the archbishop had died, but he imposed suitable penances on the accomplices in the archbishop's crimes.

Peter became ill while traveling back to his monastery from Ravenna. He made it to a monastery outside Faenza, where he died on the eighth day of his illness, with the monks gathered around him saying the Divine Office. It was February 22, 1072.

Peter was declared a Doctor of the Church by Pope Leo XII in 1828. The Church celebrates his feast on February 21.

From the Life of Saint Romuald, by Saint Peter Damian

Romuald lived in the vicinity of the city of Parenzo for three years. In the first year he built a monastery and appointed an abbot with monks. For the next two years he remained there in seclusion. In that setting, divine holiness transported him to such a summit of perfection that, breathed upon by the Holy Spirit, he foresaw many future events and comprehended with the rays of his intelligence hidden mysteries of the Old and New Testaments.

Frequently he was seized by so great a contemplation of divinity that he would be reduced to tears with the boiling, indescribable heat of divine love. In this condition he would cry out: "Beloved Jesus, beloved, sweet honey, indescribable longing, delight of the saints, sweetness of angels," and other things of this kind. We are unable to express the ecstasy of these utterances, dictated by the Holy Spirit.

Wherever the holy man might arrange to live, he would follow the same pattern. First he would build an oratory with an altar in a cell; then he would shut himself in and forbid access.

Finally, after he had lived in many places, perceiving that his end was near, he returned to the monastery he had built in the valley of Castro. While he awaited with certainty his approaching death, he ordered a cell to be constructed there with an oratory in which he might isolate himself and preserve silence until death.

Accordingly the hermitage was built, since he had made up his mind that he would die there. His body began to grow more and more oppressed by afflictions and was already failing, not so much from weakness as from the exhaustion of great age. One day he began to feel the loss of his physical strength under all the harassment of increasingly violent afflictions. As the sun was beginning to set, he instructed two monks who were standing by to go out and close the door of the cell behind them; they were to come back to him at daybreak to celebrate matins.

They were so concerned about his end that they went out reluctantly and did not rest immediately. On the contrary, since they were worried that their master might die, they lay hidden near the cell and watched this precious treasure. For some time they continued to listen attentively until they heard neither movement nor sound. Rightly guessing what had happened, they pushed open the door, rushed in quickly, lit a candle and found the holy man lying on his back, his blessed soul snatched up into heaven. As he lay there, he seemed like a neglected heavenly pearl that was soon to be given a place of honor in the treasury of the King of kings.

From a Letter by Saint Peter Damian

You asked me to write you some words of consolation, my brother. Embittered by so many tribulations, you are seeking some comfort for your soul. You asked me to offer you some soothing suggestions.

But there is no need for me to write. Consolation is already within your reach, if your good sense has not been dulled. "My son, come to the service of God. Stand in justice and fear. Prepare your soul; it is about to be tested." These words of Scripture show that you are a son of God and, as such, should take possession of your inheritance. What could be clearer than this exhortation?

Where there is justice as well as fear, adversity will surely test the spirit. But it is not the torment of a slave. Rather it is the discipline of a child by its parent.

Even in the midst of his many sufferings, the holy man Job could say: "Whip me, crush me, cut me in slices!" And he would always add: "This at least would bring me relief, yet my persecutor does not spare me."

But for God's chosen ones there is great comfort; the torment lasts but a short time. Then God bends down, cradles the fallen figure, whispers words of consolation. With hope in his heart, man picks himself up and walks again toward the glory of happiness in heaven.

Craftsmen exemplify this same practice. By hammering gold, the smith beats down the dross. The sculptor files metal to reveal a shining vein underneath. "The potter's furnace puts vessels to the test. And the fire of suffering tests the mettle of just men." The apostle James echoes this thought: "Think it a great joy, dear brothers and sisters, when you stumble onto the many kinds of trials and tribulations."

When men suffer pain for the evil they have

perpetrated in life, they should take some reassurance. They also know that for their good deeds undying rewards await them in the life to come. Therefore, my brother, scorned as you are by men, lashed as it were by God, do not despair. Do not be depressed. Do not let your weakness make you impatient. Instead, let the serenity of your spirit shine through your face. Let the joy of your mind burst forth. Let words of thanks break from your lips.

The way that God deals with men can only be praised. He lashes them in this life to shield them from the eternal lash in the next. He pins people down now; at a later time he will raise them up. He cuts them before healing; he throws them down to raise them anew.

The Scriptures reassure us: let your understanding strengthen your patience. In serenity look forward to the joy that follows sadness. Hope leads you to that joy and love enkindles your zeal. The well-prepared mind forgets the suffering inflicted from without and glides eagerly to what it has contemplated within itself.

From a Sermon on the Feast of Saint George, by Saint Peter Damian

Dear brothers and sisters, our joy in today's feast is heightened by our joy in the glory of Easter, just as the splendor of a precious jewel enhances the beauty of its gold setting. Saint George was a man who abandoned one army for another: he gave up the rank of tribune to enlist as a soldier for Christ. Eager to encounter the enemy, he first stripped away his worldly wealth by giving all he had to the poor. Then, free and unencumbered, bearing the shield of faith, he plunged into the thick of the battle, an ardent soldier for Christ.

Clearly what he did serves to teach us a valuable lesson: if we are afraid to strip ourselves of our worldly possessions, then we are unfit to make a strong defense of the faith.

As for Saint George, he was consumed with the fire of the Holy Spirit. Armed with the invincible standard of the cross, he did battle with an evil king and acquitted himself so well that, in vanquishing the king, he overcame the prince of all wicked spirits, and encouraged other soldiers of Christ to perform brave deeds in his cause.

Of course, the supreme invisible arbiter was there, who sometimes permits evil men to prevail so that his will may be accomplished. And although he surrendered the body of his martyr into the hands of murderers, yet he continued to take care of his soul, which was supported by the unshakable defense of its faith.

Dear brothers and sisters, let us not only admire the courage of this fighter in heaven's army but follow his example. Let us be inspired to strive for the reward of heavenly glory, keeping in mind his example, so that we will not be swayed from our path, though the world seduce us with its smiles or try to terrify us with naked threats of its trials and tribulations.

We must now cleanse ourselves, as Saint Paul tells us, from all defilement of body and spirit, so that one day we too may deserve to enter that temple of blessedness to which we now aspire.

Anyone who wishes to offer himself to God in the tent of Christ, which is the Church, must first bathe in the spring of holy baptism; then he must put on the various garments of the virtues. As it says in the Scriptures: "Let your priests be clothed in justice." He who is reborn in baptism is a new man. He may no longer wear the things that signify mortality. He has discarded the old self and must put on the new. He must live continually renewed in his commitment to a holy sojourn in this world.

Truly we must be cleansed of the stains of our past sins and be resplendent in the virtue of our new way of life. Then we can be confident of celebrating Easter worthily and of truly following the example of the blessed martyrs.

CHAPTER 19

SAINT ANSELM

Saint Anselm is known as "the Father of Scholasticism" for his efforts to analyze and illumine the truths of faith through the aid of reason. He is considered the most important philosopher and theologian between Saint Augustine and Saint Thomas Aquinas.

Since he was an archbishop of Canterbury, Anselm is usually thought of as British, but he was actually Italian or French, being born to French noble parents in Aosta, northern Italy, about the year 1033. His parents were Gundolf and Ermenberga from an old Burgundian family. He was deeply influenced by his pious mother and at age fifteen asked to be admitted to a monastery. His father, though, was opposed and the abbot, well aware of that opposition, refused to admit him. Anselm, then, unable to enter a monastery, lost interest in religion and began to lead the life of a carefree young nobleman.

Gundolf was always stern with Anselm, to such an extent that when Ermenberga, his mother, died, Anselm was virtually forced to leave home. He moved to Burgundy, France, where he studied for a time and then entered a school at Bec in Normandy, France. He was there when his father died and he was torn between returning to Italy to manage the estates he inherited or entering a monastery as he wanted to do at age fifteen. Archbishop Maurillus of Rouen advised him to become a monk, so Anselm entered the Benedictine monastery at Bec when he was twenty-seven. The great churchman Lanfranc was abbot at the time. When, three years later, Lanfranc was also made abbot of St. Stephen's in nearby Caen, Anselm was appointed prior at Bec.

It was while he was prior at Bec that Anselm did some of his greatest writing, especially works of metaphysics. He wanted to satisfy his mind that God really existed and to offer rational proofs for his existence. Not that he ever doubted. He wrote, "I do not seek to understand in order to believe, but I believe in order to understand." His first work was his *Monologion*, in which he restated all the logical arguments he could find in writings by other theologians that God truly exists. Then he wrote his *Proslogion*, offering original proofs of his own and contemplation of God's attributes. He also wrote treatises on truth, free will, the origin of evil, and a work on the art of reasoning.

Besides his writings, Anselm was also respected for his teaching skills, which he tried to instill in the other monks. Soon the Abbey of Bec had a reputation for being an excellent monastic school.

In 1078, after Anselm had been prior at Bec for fifteen years, Lanfranc was appointed archbishop of Canterbury and Anselm was unanimously chosen as abbot at Bec. His duties required him to cross the English Channel to visit extensive properties in England that the abbey owned. This gave him a first-hand knowledge of the difficulties Lanfranc was having with William the Conqueror, then known as King William I. The king continually interfered with Church affairs until his death in 1087. He was succeeded by King William Rufus.

Lanfranc died in 1089 and the king decided to keep the see of Canterbury vacant so that he could retain the episcopal revenues for himself. In 1092, Anselm accepted an invitation to go to England to advise the Earl of Chester about a monastery he proposed to build. That business, plus other matters in connection with the property the Bec abbey owned, kept Anselm in England for five months. During that time, King William Rufus became seriously ill and almost died. During his illness he became frightened enough to change his mind about keeping the see of Canterbury vacant and, when he recovered, nominated Anselm to be its archbishop. Anselm tried to refuse but when he tried to return to France he was restrained by order of the king. Then the English bishops told

him that, if he declined, all that was wrong in
Church-State affairs would be his responsibility.
They forced the pastoral staff into his hands.
Anselm finally agreed to be archbishop of Canter-
bury and was consecrated on December 4, 1093,
at age sixty.

Soon, though, relations between king and
archbishop deteriorated. The king demanded a
large sum of money as the price of Anselm's nomi-
nation to the see, and Anselm flatly refused. And
when Anselm urged the king to fill vacant offices
in abbeys and to sanction the convening of Church
synods to correct abuses among the clergy and
laity, King William refused. He not only refused,
but he took steps to try to deprive Anselm of the
see of Canterbury. He even tried to get Pope Urban II to depose Anselm by promising an annual
tribute to the Holy See.

Anselm decided to take the Church-State
problems to the pope and twice requested permission to travel to Rome. At first King William refused to let him leave, but finally told him that he
could go if he wanted but if he did his revenues
would be confiscated and he would never be allowed to return. Anselm went anyway, taking the
long trip from England to Rome in 1097. There the
pope assured him of his protection and wrote to
King William, demanding that he reinstate Anselm
in all his rights and responsibilities.

Unable to return to England, Anselm found

a quiet retreat in a monastery in Italy and resumed his writing. He completed his book *Cur Deus Homo*, or *Why God Became Man*, in which he explained the wisdom, justice, and necessity of the Incarnation.

Anselm was still in Italy when the regional Council of Bari was held in 1098 to try to bring about a reconciliation between the Eastern and Western Churches. Pope Urban II invited him to attend. The story has been told that, during a heated discussion over whether the Holy Spirit proceeded from the Father only (as the Greek Church claimed) or from the Father and the Son (as the Latin Church claimed), the pope suddenly called out, "Anselm, our father and master, where are you?" Anselm hurried to the pope's side and the pope asked him to speak on the issue. Anselm did the next day and delivered such a convincing discourse that the dispute over the issue was ended. (It was later revived and remains today a theological difference between the Catholic and Orthodox Churches.)

The council also denounced King William for simony, for persecuting Anselm, for oppression of the Church, and for personal depravity. Only entreaties by Anselm prevented the pope from excommunicating the king. But the threat was there.

After the Council of Bari, Anselm returned to France, where he stayed in Lyons. There he wrote a treatise *On Original Sin*.

King William Rufus died in 1100 and his brother and successor, Henry I, invited Anselm to return to his see at Canterbury. Anselm returned after an absence of three years. But tensions between him and Henry began almost immediately when Henry wanted to reinvest Anselm as archbishop. A Roman synod just the previous year had forbidden lay investiture and Anselm refused. The matter was referred to the pope.

Meanwhile, King Henry needed Anselm's help because Robert of Normandy was threatening to invade England. Henry promised obedience to the Holy See in return for Anselm's support. When Robert actually did land with an army at Portsmouth, Anselm denounced the English barons who sided with Robert and excommunicated Robert as an invader. This compelled Robert to come to terms with the king and return to Normandy.

Once the crisis was over, King Henry renewed his claim to the right of nominating and investing bishops. Anselm, though, refused to consecrate any bishops nominated by the king unless they were canonically elected. As the dispute between king and archbishop widened, Anselm decided once again to travel to Rome to present the matter to the pope, who by this time was Paschal II. The pope sided with Anselm. King Henry then sent word that Anselm was forbidden to return to England and that all his revenues were confiscated.

Anselm then threatened to excommunicate the king, and this threat seems to have alarmed King Henry enough that some sort of reconciliation resulted.

Again Anselm returned to Canterbury and Henry restored the revenues of his see. Then, at a royal council of clergy and barons in 1107, the king renounced the right of investiture to bishoprics or abbeys. In return, Anselm agreed that English bishops could do homage to the king with their temporal possessions. King Henry came to regard Anselm so highly that, in 1108, while the king was in France, he made Anselm regent.

In addition to his theological writings, Anselm is also notable for being among the first people to take a stand against the slave trade. In 1102, at a national council in Westminster, he obtained the passage of a resolution against the practice of selling men like cattle.

Anselm died on Wednesday of Holy Week, April 21, 1109, in his seventy-sixth year, and was buried in Canterbury Cathedral. (His shrine there was later destroyed by King Henry VIII.) He was declared a Doctor of the Church in 1720 by Pope Clement XI. The Church celebrates his feast on April 21.

Excerpts from the *Proslogion*, by Saint Anselm

Insignificant man, escape from your everyday business for a short while, hide for a moment from your restless thoughts. Break off from your cares and troubles and be less concerned about your tasks and labors. Make a little time for God and rest a while in him.

Enter into your mind's inner chamber. Shut out everything but God and whatever helps you to seek him; and when you have shut the door, look for him. Speak now to God and say with your whole heart: "I seek your face; your face, Lord, I desire."

Lord, my God, teach my heart where and how to seek you, where and how to find you. Lord, if you are not here, where shall I look for you in your absence? Yet if you are everywhere, why do I not see you when you are present? But surely you dwell in "light inaccessible." And where is light inaccessible? How shall I approach light inaccessible? Or who will lead me and bring me into it that I may see you there? And then, by what signs and under what forms shall I seek you? I have never seen you, Lord my God; I do not know your face.

Lord most high, what shall this exile do, so far from you? What shall your servant do, tormented by love of you and cast so far from your face? He yearns to see you, and your face is too far from him. He desires to approach you, and your dwelling is unapproachable. He longs to find you, and does not know your dwelling place. He strives to look for you, and does not know your face.

Lord, you are my God and you are my Lord, and I have never seen you. You have made me and remade me, and you have given me all the good things I possess, and still I do not know you. I was made in order to see you, and I have not yet done that for which I was made.

Lord, how long will it be? How long, Lord, will you forget us? How long will you turn your face away from us? When will you look upon us and hear us? When will you enlighten our eyes and show us your face? When will you give yourself back to us?

Look upon us, Lord, hear us and enlighten us, show us your very self. Restore yourself to us that it may go well with us whose life is so evil without you. Take pity on our efforts and our striving toward you, for we have no strength apart from you.

Teach me to seek you, and when I seek you show yourself to me, for I cannot seek you unless you teach me, nor can I find you unless you show yourself to me. Let me seek you in desiring you and desire you in seeking you, find you in loving you and love you in finding you. Lord, I acknowledge and thank you that you have created me in your image, in order that I may be mindful of you, conceive of you and love you. But that image has been so consumed and wasted away by vices, and obscured by the smoke of wrongdoing that it cannot achieve that for which it was created except you renew it and create it anew.

I do not endeavor, Lord, to penetrate your heights, for in no way do I compare my understanding with yours; but I long to understand in some degree your truth which my heart believes and loves. For I do not seek to understand in order that I may believe, but I believe in order to understand. For this also I believe — that unless I believe I shall not understand.

* * *

And so, Lord, do you, who gives understanding to faith, give me, so far as you know it to be profitable, to understand that you are as we believe, and that you are what we believe. And we believe that you are a being than whom nothing greater can be conceived. Or is there no such being, since "the fool has said in his heart, there is no God"? But at least this same fool, when he hears of this being of whom I speak — a being than whom nothing greater can be conceived — understands what he hears and what he understands is in his understanding, although he does not understand it to exist.

For it is one thing to conceive an object as in the understanding, and another to understand that the object exists. When a painter first conceives what he will afterwards paint he has it in his understanding but does not yet understand it to exist, because he has not yet painted it. But after he has finished the picture, he both has it in his understanding and understands that it exists, because he has painted it.

Hence even the fool knows that something exists in the understanding, at least, than which nothing greater can be conceived. For when he hears of it, he understands it, and whatever is understood exists in the understanding. But assuredly that than which nothing greater can be conceived cannot exist in the understanding alone. For suppose it exists in the understanding alone, then it can be conceived to exist in reality, which is greater.

* * *

And assuredly it exists so truly that it cannot be conceived not to exist. For it is possible to conceive of a being which cannot be conceived as non-existing; and it is greater than one which can be conceived as non-existing. Hence if that than which nothing greater can be conceived can be conceived as non-existing, it is not that than which nothing greater can be conceived. But this is an irreconcilable contradiction. There is then so truly a being than which nothing greater can be conceived to exist that it cannot even be conceived as non-existent. And this being you are, O Lord.

So truly, therefore, you do exist, O Lord my God, that you cannot be conceived as non-existent, and rightly. For if a mind could conceive of a being better than you, the creature would rise above its Creator, which is utterly absurd.

* * *

My soul, have you found what you are looking for? You were looking for God, and you have discovered that he is the supreme being, and that you could not possibly imagine anything more perfect. You have discovered that this supreme being is life itself, light, wisdom, goodness, eternal blessedness and blessed eternity. He is everywhere, and he is timeless.

Lord my God, you gave me life and restored it when I lost it. Tell my soul that so longs for you what else you are besides what it has already understood, so that it may see you clearly. It stands on tiptoe to see more, but apart from what it has seen already, it sees nothing but darkness. Of course it does not really see darkness, because there is no darkness in you, but it sees that it can see no further because of the darkness in itself.

Surely, Lord, inaccessible light is your dwelling place, for no one apart from yourself can enter into it and fully comprehend you. If I fail to see this light it is simply because it is too bright for me. Still, it is by this light that I do see all that

I can, even as weak eyes, unable to look straight at the sun, see all that they can by the sun's light.

The light in which you dwell, Lord, is beyond my understanding. It is so brilliant that I cannot bear it, I cannot turn my mind's eye toward it for any length of time. I am dazzled by its brightness, amazed by its grandeur, overwhelmed by its immensity, bewildered by its abundance.

O supreme and inaccessible light, O complete and blessed truth, how far you are from me, even though I am so near to you! How remote you are from my sight, even though I am present to yours! You are everywhere in your entirety, and yet I do not see you; in you I move and have my being, and yet I cannot approach you; you are within me and around me, and yet I do not perceive you.

O God, let me know you and love you so that I may find my joy in you; and if I cannot do so fully in this life, let me at least make some progress every day, until at last that knowledge, love and joy come to me in all their plenitude. While I am here on earth let me learn to know you better, so that in heaven I may know you fully; let my love for you grow deeper here, so that there I may love you fully. On earth then I shall have great joy in hope, and in heaven complete joy in the fulfillment of my hope.

O Lord, through your Son you command us, no, you counsel us to ask, and you promise that you will hear us so that our joy may be complete. Lord, I am making the request that you urge us to make through your Wonder-Counselor. Give me then what you promise to give through your Truth. You, O God, are faithful; grant that I may receive my request, so that my joy may be complete.

Meanwhile, let this hope of mine be in my thoughts and on my tongue; let my heart be filled with it, my voice speak of it; let my soul hunger for it, my body thirst for it, my whole being yearn for it, until I enter into the joy of the Lord, who is Three in One, blessed for ever. Amen.

CHAPTER 20

SAINT BERNARD OF CLAIRVAUX

Beyond a doubt, Saint Bernard was the outstanding churchman of the twelfth century. He was an eloquent preacher (called the "Mellifluous or Honey-sweet Doctor"), reformer of a monastic order, Scripture scholar, adviser to popes and princes, healer of a schism, battler against heresy, and preacher of the Second Crusade. Yet all he really wanted to do was to be hidden from the world in the walls of a Cistercian monastery.

Bernard was born to wealth, in his family's castle of Fontaines, near Dijon in Burgundy, in 1091. He was the third of seven children — six boys and one girl — of Tescelin and Aleth Sorrel. His mother saw to her children's education as well as their training in spirituality. Bernard was sent to Chatillon-on-the-Seine, completing his studies at about the age of nineteen. While he was at school, his mother's death threw him into a state of prolonged and acute depression.

His leadership abilities and eloquence were

demonstrated when he decided to enter a Cistercian monastery at Citeaux when he was twenty-two. He convinced no fewer than thirty-one men to enter with him, including all of his brothers except Nivard, the youngest. It was reported that, as the men prepared to ride away, Guy, the eldest brother, said, "Farewell, little Nivard! You will have all our lands and estates for yourself." The young boy replied, "Oh, then you are taking heaven and leaving me only the earth! The division is too unequal!" (Later both Nivard and the brothers' father also became Cistercians and received their habits from Bernard's hands.)

The men traveled together and arrived at Citeaux around Easter of 1112. The monastery's abbot, Stephen Harding, hadn't had a novice for several years, so he received them with open arms. At the end of a year, all but one made their profession of vows. When Bernard was twenty-five, Abbot Stephen ordered him to take twelve monks, including his brothers, and found a new Cistercian house in Champagne with Bernard as abbot. They settled in the Valley of Wormwood where they cleared a piece of land and built a plain dwelling.

At first, Bernard was quite severe in his discipline with the other monks and they began to get discouraged. Realizing his fault, he imposed on himself a long silence until he was bidden by a vision to start preaching again. As the fame of the house and its holy abbot spread through that part of France, the number of monks grew to one hundred thirty. The monastery and the valley were given the name Clairvaux, the valley of light, because they were situated in the eye of the sun.

Although Bernard wanted nothing more than to remain in his monastery, obedience and the needs of the Church frequently drew him from his cell. His reputation for learning and sanctity and his talent as a mediator became so famous that princes called on him to decide their disputes, bishops asked his opinion on problems involving their churches, and popes accepted his counsel.

In 1130 a full-blown schism rocked the Church upon the death of Pope Honorius II. Innocent II was chosen pope by a majority of the cardinals, but a minority faction elected a cardinal who took the name Anacletus II. Anacletus managed to control the city of Rome and Innocent fled to Pisa. A council of bishops was held soon afterwards and Bernard was asked to attend. As a result of his vigorous efforts, Innocent was recognized as the legitimate pope. Bernard then traveled with Pope Innocent to meet with the rulers of Europe and win their support. He then accompanied the pope in a triumphant march back to Rome. Anacletus, though, continued to claim the papacy until his death in 1138. His supporters elected a successor, Victor IV, but, as a result of Bernard's preaching in Rome, Victor submitted to Pope Innocent only two months after his election.

Bernard was recognized as the most eloquent and influential man of his age. Next to him in stature was the brilliant teacher Peter Abelard, who was a greater scholar than Bernard. However, Peter Abelard's orthodoxy was questioned and a synod had condemned his book about the Trinity in 1121. Nevertheless, he continued to teach in Paris. In 1139 the Cistercian William of Saint Thierry denounced him as a heretic and asked Bernard to try to bring Abelard around to orthodox teachings since he thought Bernard was the only man able to do so. Bernard met with Abelard three times, but Abelard continued in his error. Finally a council at Sens in 1141 charged Abelard with heresy. Bernard, at first reluctant to testify, finally did so and refuted Abelard's teachings. The bishops at the council condemned as heretical seventeen propositions taken from Abelard's writings. Abelard died shortly afterward. Bernard has been criticized for his uncompromising attitude but he felt that Abelard's brilliance made him extremely dangerous for the Christian faith.

In 1139 Bernard attended the 10th ecumenical council, the Second Council of the Lateran, which approved 30 canons related to discipline and other matters, one of which stated that holy orders is an invalidating impediment to marriage. When people say that clerical celibacy has been a law of the Church only since the 12th century, this is what they have in mind. While at the council,

Bernard met Malachy, the bishop of Armagh, Ireland, with whom he established a close friendship. Malachy took a number of young men with him to be trained by Bernard and in 1142 the first Cistercian monastery was established in Ireland. Later Malachy retired from the see of Armagh and moved to Clairvaux, where he died in Bernard's arms.

In 1138, during the time that Bernard was preaching on behalf of Pope Innocent II, a young man named Peter Bernard Paganelli joined the monastery at Clairvaux. In 1142 Peter Bernard was elected pope, taking the name Eugenius III. Bernard naturally felt a fatherly concern for the new pope and wrote a treatise for him called *On Consideration*. It elaborated on the proper duties of the pontiff and the problems facing him in the papal government. It reminded Eugenius to reserve time every day for self examination and contemplation, a duty that Bernard said was more vital than any official business. It is considered to be one of Bernard's most important works.

Meanwhile, in the south of France, the Albigensian heresy had been making alarming progress. This heresy taught that all matter was created by evil, while the spirit was created by goodness. It taught that Christ's death and resurrection were only allegorical and that he was actually an angel. The Albigensian form of religious austerity was attractive to many people so, in 1145, the papal legate to France, Cardinal Alberic, asked Bernard to go to Languedoc to combat the heresy. Although he was in alarmingly poor health at the time, Bernard obeyed and in a short time it appeared that he had been able to restore orthodoxy. However, twenty-five years later the Albigensians were stronger than ever and St. Dominic was sent to win back the country once more.

In another part of the world, the Holy Land, the Seljuk Turks were fighting against the Christians. When they captured Edessa on Christmas Day of 1144, appeals went up for help. The pope asked Bernard to preach throughout Europe on behalf of organizing a new crusade, which became the Second Crusade. Bernard obeyed and wrote to the rulers of France, England, Italy, Sicily, Spain, Poland, Denmark, Moravia, Bohemia and Bavaria, and went in person to Germany, encouraging them to send troops for the crusade. Bernard's eloquence was so convincing that a vast army was assembled.

The Second Crusade was a miserable failure, ending in a complete military and moral disaster. The Crusaders did not have the commitment Bernard had and committed every sort of sordid act along the way. Some believe that the failure of the crusade hastened Bernard's death, although he had been in ill health for most of his life.

Bernard died on August 20, 1153. He was sixty-three years old, had been abbot for thirty-eight years, and had seen sixty-eight monasteries established by his men from Clairvaux. He wrote more than three hundred letters and sermons and other mystical treatises and he is known particularly for his sermons "On the Song of Songs" and for his devotion to the Blessed Virgin Mary.

He was canonized in 1174, twenty-one years after his death, and Pope Pius VIII named him a Doctor of the Church in 1830. His feast is celebrated on August 20.

From a Sermon on the Song of Songs, by St. Bernard

Where can the weak find a place of firm security and peace, except in the wounds of the Savior? Indeed, the more secure is my place there, the more he can do to help me. The world rages, the flesh is heavy, and the devil lays his snares, but I do not fall, for my feet are planted on firm rock. I may have sinned gravely. My conscience would be distressed, but it would not be in turmoil, for I would recall the wounds of the Lord: "He was wounded for our iniquities." What sin is there so deadly that it cannot be pardoned by the death of Christ? And so if I bear in mind this strong, effective remedy, I can never again be terrified by the malignancy of sin.

Surely the man who said: "My sin is too great to merit pardon," was wrong. He was speaking as though he were not a member of Christ and had no share in his merits, so that he could claim them as his own, as a member of the body can claim what belongs to the head. As for me, what can I appropriate that I lack from the heart of the Lord who abounds in mercy? They pierced his hands and feet and opened his side with a spear. Through the openings of these wounds I may drink "honey from the rock and oil from the hardest stone": that is, I may "taste and see that the Lord is sweet."

He was thinking thoughts of peace, and I did not know it, "for who knows the mind of the Lord, or who has been his counselor?" But the piercing nail has become a key to unlock the door, that I may see the good will of the Lord. And what can I see as I look through the hole? Both the nail and the wound cry out that God was in Christ reconciling the world to himself. "The sword pierced his soul and came close to his heart," so that he might be able to feel compassion for me in my weaknesses.

Through these sacred wounds we can see the secret of his heart, the great mystery of love, "the sincerity of his mercy with which he visited us from on high." Where have your love, your mercy, your compassion shone out more luminously than in your wounds, sweet, gentle Lord of mercy? More mercy than this no one has than that he lay down his life for those who are doomed to death.

My merit comes from his mercy; for I do not

lack merit so long as he does not lack pity. And if the Lord's mercies are many, then I am rich in merits. For even if I am aware of many sins, what does it matter? "Where sin abounded grace has overflowed." And if "the Lord's mercies are from all ages forever," I too "will sing of the mercies of the Lord forever." Will I not sing of my own righteousness? No, "Lord, I shall be mindful only of your justice." Yet that too is my own; for God has made you my righteousness.

From a Homily in Praise of the Virgin Mother, by St. Bernard

It was fitting that the Virgin should give birth only to God; and it was also fitting that God should be born only of the Virgin. Accordingly, the Creator of mankind, in order that he might become a man by being born of a human being, had to seek out from among all mankind and designate as his mother a woman he knew would be worthy of him and pleasing to him. And so he chose a sinless virgin, that he might be born sinless and free of all stain. He chose a humble virgin, from whom he might come forth meek and humble of heart, to display a most necessary and salutary model of these virtues for all mankind. Thus he allowed a virgin to conceive, in whom he had earlier inspired a vow of virginity, and required of her the merit of humility.

Otherwise how could the angel afterward pronounce her full of grace, if she had the slightest good quality which did not come from grace? Thus she, who was to conceive and bring forth the holy of holies, must be sanctified physically and so she received the gift of virginity; that she might be sanctified spiritually, she received the gift of humility.

The Virgin then, adorned like a queen with the jewels of virtue, shone with the glory of body and soul; and seen on high as radiantly beautiful, she so attracted the inhabitants of heaven that she moved the heart of the King with desire for her and brought down from above the heavenly message. Scripture says: "The angel was sent to a virgin." For she was truly virgin in body, virgin in mind, a virgin by her special calling, sanctified, as the Apostle reminds us, in both mind and body. This came about by no unforeseen or accidental occurrence; she was chosen from eternity, foreknown and prepared by the Most High for himself, guarded by the angels, prefigured by the patriarchs, and promised by the prophets.

From a Sermon on Guardian Angels, by St. Bernard

"He has given his angels charge over you to guard you in all your ways. Let them thank the Lord for his mercy; his wonderful works are for the children of men." Let them give thanks and say among the nations, the Lord has done great things for them. O Lord, what is man that you made yourself known to him, or why do you incline your heart to him? And you do incline your heart to him; you show him your care and your concern. Finally, you send your only Son and the grace of your Spirit, and promise him a vision of your countenance. And so, that nothing in heaven should be wanting in your concern for us, you send those blessed spirits to serve us, assigning them as our guardians.

"He has given his angels charge over you to guard you in all your ways." These words should fill you with respect, inspire devotion and instill confidence; respect for the presence of angels, devotion because of their loving service, and confidence because of their protection. And so the angels are here; they are at your side, they are with you, present on your behalf. They are here to protect you and to serve you. But even if it is God who has given them this charge, we must nonetheless be grateful to them for the great love with which they obey and come to help us in our great need. So let us be devoted and grateful to such great protectors; let us return their love and honor them as much as we can and should. Yet all our love and honor must go to him for it is from him that they receive all that makes them worthy of our love and respect.

We should then, my brothers, show our affection for the angels, for one day they will be our coheirs just as here below they are our guardians and trustees appointed and set over us by the Father. We are God's children although it does not seem so, because we are still but small children under guardians and trustees, and for the present little better than slaves.

Even though we are children and have a long, a very long and dangerous way to go, with such protectors what have we to fear? They who keep us in all our ways cannot be overpowered or led astray. They are loyal, prudent, powerful. Why then are we afraid? We have only to follow them, stay close to them, and we shall dwell under the protection of God's heaven.

From *The Book on the Love of God,* by Saint Bernard

You wish me to tell you why God should be loved, and in what way or measure we should love him. I answer then: the reason for our loving God *is* God; and measure of that love there should be none.

Is that enough to say about the matter? For a wise man most probably it is, but I am under obligation to the foolish also; and though I may have said enough for those with understanding, I must have due regard for others too. For those less apt, then, I gladly will explain what I have said more fully, if not with greater depth.

I might have said there was a twofold reason for loving God solely for himself. First: nothing can be loved more justly. And, second: nothing can be loved with so much profit to ourselves. The question *Why should God be loved?* includes both of these, for it may mean either *What is his claim upon our love?* or *What benefit shall we derive from loving him?*

My former answer stands in either case; there is no other worthy cause for loving God except himself. As to his claim upon our love, he surely merits much from us who gave himself to us, unworthy as we were: what better gift *could* he have given than himself? If, then, it is his claim we have in mind when asking, *Why should God be loved?* the first and foremost answer is, "Because he first loved us."

Most plainly is he worthy of our answering love, especially if we consider who he is who thus bestows his love on us, who are the objects of it, and how great it is. For who is he, save he whom every soul confesses, "You are my God, my goods are nothing unto you"? His is indeed the sovereign charity, that seeks for nothing for itself.

But who are they to whom he shows this selfless love? "When we were enemies," the Apostle says, "we were reconciled to God." God, then, has loved us freely, while we were enemies.

How much has he loved us? John says, "God loved the world so much that he gave his only-begotten Son."

"He spared not his only Son," says Paul, "but delivered him up for us all."

The Son moreover tells us of himself, "Greater love has no man than this, that a man lay down his life for his friends." This is the claim the Just One has on sinners, the Highest on the lowest, and he who is Almighty on the weak.

Chapter 21

SAINT ANTHONY OF PADUA

When you consider that Saint Anthony of Padua died when he was only thirty-six, it's amazing that he was able to cram as much into his life as he did, or that such a young man could achieve the acclaim that he did.

Since he is so closely connected with the northern Italian city of Padua, it's easy to assume that he was Italian. But he was born in Lisbon, Portugal to a noble Portuguese family, and he was baptized with the name Ferdinand. His parents enrolled him in the cathedral school in Lisbon and when he was fifteen he joined the Canons Regular of Saint Augustine. They were the clergy who were attached to the cathedral who lived together under a monastic rule devised by Saint Augustine. (See the chapter on Saint Augustine in the first volume of this work.)

When Ferdinand was seventeen, he asked to be transferred to the priory of Santa Croce in Coimbra (then the capital of Portugal) in order to avoid the distractions of friends in Lisbon. He was at Coimbra for eight years, devoting himself to study and prayer. It was during those eight years that he acquired a thorough knowledge of Scripture.

In 1220, when Ferdinand was twenty-five, Don Pedro, the crown prince of Portugal, brought back from Morocco the relics of some Franciscan missionaries who had recently been martyred. Seeing those relics and hearing the story of the martyrs affected Ferdinand profoundly, and he felt an ardent desire to die for his faith. Since there was no possibility of that while he was a Canon Regular, he spoke to some Franciscans who came by his monastery to beg, and they encouraged him to join their order. Although his superiors objected to this move, he finally received permission and received the Franciscan habit in the chapel of St. Anthony of Olivares in 1221. The chapel was dedicated to St. Anthony of Egypt and Ferdinand changed his own name to Anthony in honor of this hermit-saint.

The Franciscans gladly permitted Anthony to embark for Morocco on a mission to preach Christianity to the Moors. But he no sooner arrived there than he was afflicted with a severe illness, and he had to return to Europe. However, the ship in which he sailed for Portugal was blown off course by a storm and landed at Messina, Sicily. While in Sicily he recovered his health. He also learned that the Franciscans were planning a general chapter at Assisi. It was the last such chapter open to all members of the order, presided over by Brother Elias, the new vicar general, with Saint Francis present. Anthony sailed to Italy and attended the chapter meetings.

At the end of the chapter, the Franciscan provincial ministers made new assignments. Since there was no Portuguese provincial, Anthony found himself assigned to Brother Gratian, the provincial of Romagna, which comprised the whole of Lombardy. Brother Gratian sent Anthony to the lonely hermitage of San Paolo, near Forli, where he was given menial tasks such as washing the dishes and cooking pots after meals.

It happened that an ordination of both Franciscans and Dominicans was scheduled for Forli, with a celebration afterwards at the Franciscan convent. Through a lack of communication, neither the Dominicans nor the Franciscans had assigned anyone to deliver the customary address. At the awkward moment, Anthony's superior told him to go forward and speak whatever the Holy Spirit might inspire him to say. Sheepishly, Anthony obeyed. But once he was standing in front of his audience, he delivered such a brilliant and eloquent address that it surprised everyone present. His superiors had no inkling that Anthony had this talent. His years of studying Scripture had prepared him to allow the Holy Spirit to use his talents.

Brother Gratian, informed of Anthony's talent, was quick to use Anthony. He sent him out to preach in the cities of the province, and he was an immediate success. Then, since he was so well versed in theology, he was given another assignment: In addition to his work as an itinerant preacher he was appointed reader in theology to the Franciscans, the first person to fill such a position. Francis himself wrote to him: "To my dearest brother Anthony, brother Francis sends greetings in Jesus Christ. I am well pleased that you should read sacred theology to the friars, provided that such study does not quench the spirit of holy prayer and devotion according to our rule."

At the time several heretical sects were threatening the Church, especially the Cathars in Italy and the Albigensians in France. Both were neo-Manichaeans who rejected the sacraments and Church authority. Anthony preached against the Cathars in Italy from 1222 to 1224 and against the Albigensians in France from 1224 to 1226 while also teaching theology in the universities of Bologna, Montpellier and Toulouse. Because of his success in preaching against heresies, he became widely known as "Hammer of Heretics."

The Franciscans also used him in administrative positions — guardian or prior at one monastery and custodian at another. Then Saint Francis died on October 3, 1226. Shortly after that, the Franciscans held another general chapter, which Anthony attended. It appears that the Franciscans wanted Anthony to become a provincial minister. But, after the chapter ended, he was sent as an envoy to Pope Gregory IX, to inform him of the various conflicts that arose at the discordant chapter. Anthony used the occasion to ask the pope to excuse him from holding any other offices in the Franciscan order so he could devote his time and energy to preaching. The pope, who had such a high regard for Anthony's familiarity with Scripture that he once referred to him as "the Ark of the Testament," agreed.

So Anthony moved to Padua in northern Italy and concentrated on the preaching in which he excelled. Besides his powers of logical analysis and reasoning, he also seemed to have a magnetic personality and a resonant voice. It has been written that the mere sight of Anthony brought sinners to their knees because he radiated a spiritual force. Crowds flocked to hear him, shop-keepers closed their shops in order to attend his sermons, and women even stayed overnight in church to have a good seat. When congregations overflowed the churches, Anthony preached in the public squares.

Soon his sermons led to a reformation of morals in Padua and the surrounding area. Quarrels were settled, owners of ill-gotten goods made restitution at Anthony's feet, and Anthony convinced the city officials to pass a law exempting from prison debtors willing to surrender all their possessions to satisfy their creditors.

Anthony was soon called "the Wonder Worker" because of reported miracles, including the restoration of a severed leg and raising a man from the dead so he could testify in a murder case. It is said that he sometimes preached to crowds in the rain but his audiences remained dry.

In the spring of 1231, after a particularly wearying series of sermons, Anthony was exhausted and went with two of the Franciscan brothers to a woodland retreat at Camposanpiero for rest. It soon became clear, though, that he was suffering from more than exhaustion, that he was dying. He asked to be taken back to Padua, but he got only as far as the convent of the Poor Clares of Arcella. In the apartment reserved for the chaplain there, he received the last rites and died on June 13, 1231. He was canonized within a year of his death and the people of Padua built a basilica in his honor in 1263. There his relics, including his vocal chords, are displayed.

Saint Anthony has been a popular saint. Statues and paintings often depict him with the Child Jesus on his arm because of the legend that once a friend glanced through the window of a house and saw Anthony with the Holy Child in his arms. He is the patron saint of Padua, Lisbon, Split, Paderborn, Hildesheim, children, travelers, married couples, women, animals, and miners. He is invoked against infertility, demons, fevers, wars, shipwrecks, and plagues.

Perhaps, though, he is best known as the finder of lost articles. It is not clear why this is so. The only story concerning Saint Anthony that seems to have anything at all to do with lost objects is contained in the *Chronicles of the Twenty-four Generals* of the Franciscan order. It says that a novice ran away from his monastery while carrying a psalter which Anthony had been using. Anthony prayed for its recovery, the novice was frightened by an apparition, and he brought it back.

Saint Anthony was declared a Doctor of the Church by Pope Pius XII in 1946. The Church celebrates his feast on June 13.

From *Sermons for the Liturgical Year*, by Saint Anthony

CHRISTMAS

"Unto us a child is born, unto us a son is given; he bears his kingship on his shoulders and his name is called Wonderful, Counselor, ... the Prince of Peace." A little above [this quotation from Isaiah], he says: "Behold, a virgin shall conceive and bear a son and his name shall be Emmanuel, that is to say, God-with-us."

God made himself for us a little child; he was born for us. Among his many titles Christ is called a little child; I shall use but this one. You have hurt a child, you have struck him, but you show him a kindness, you give him a flower, a rose, or some other object he likes. Instantly he forgets the hurt you did him, his anger is gone and he runs to embrace you. Thus it is with Christ. You have offended him by a mortal sin or wounded him by some fault, but you offer him the flower of contrition or the rose of a confession steeped in tears. Tears are the blood of the soul. At once he forgets your offense, he forgives your sin, he runs, he takes you in his arms and gives you his kiss of peace....

His name is called Wonderful, Counselor ... the Prince of Peace. In the moral sense, these words indicate the qualities of any penitent or good man. The good man is wonderful in his keen and frequent examination of his own conscience, for he sees strange things in the depths of his heart. "The anguish of his spirit" and "the bitterness of his soul," as Job says, let nothing pass by him but he scrutinizes and examines everything down to the least detail. The good man is a Counselor in the spiritual and bodily necessities of his neighbor. Like Job he says: "I am eye to the blind and foot to the lame." Blind is he who sees not his own conscience; lame is he who wanders from the right way. The good man comes to the help of each. He makes himself eye to the blind by leading him to recognize the sad state of his conscience. He makes himself foot to the lame by supporting him and guiding him into the way of righteousness and goodness.

Prince of Peace, the good man lives in a

perfect tranquillity of soul and body. As Job says, "The beasts of the field," that is, the stirring of the flesh, "leave him in peace." Unknown, dead to the world in contemplation, "he sleeps in safety and no one disturbs his rest."

THIRD SUNDAY AFTER EPIPHANY

"Jesus stretched forth his hand and touched the leper and said to him: I will: be thou clean." O, how I marvel at that hand! "That hand carved of gold, set with precious stones"; that hand whose touch loosens the tongue of the dumb man, brings back to life the daughter of Jairus, and cleanses the leper; that hand of which the prophet Isaiah speaks to us: "It alone has done all these wondrous things."

To stretch forth the hand is to bestow a gift. O Lord, stretch forth your hand, that hand which the executioner will stretch out on the cross; touch the leper and give him of your bounty! All that your hand shall touch shall be purified and healed. "He touched Malchus' ear and healed it." He stretched forth his hand to bestow on the leper the gift of health; he said: "I will: be thou clean," and immediately the leprosy was cleansed. "He does whatever he wills." In him nothing separates willing from accomplishment.

Now this instant healing God performs daily in the soul of the sinner through the ministry of the priest. The priest has a threefold office: he must stretch forth his hand, that is, pray for the sinner and take pity on him; he must touch him, console him, promise him pardon; he must will that pardon, and grant it and his absolution. Such is the threefold pastoral ministry which the Lord committed to Peter, when he said to him thrice: "Feed my sheep."

PENTECOST

The man who is filled with the Holy Spirit speaks in different languages. These different languages are different ways of witnessing to Christ, such as humility, poverty, patience and obedience; we speak in those languages when we reveal in ourselves these virtues to others.

Actions speak louder than words; let your words teach and your actions speak. We are full of words but empty of actions, and therefore are cursed by the Lord, since he himself cursed the fig tree when he found no fruit but only leaves. [Saint] Gregory [the Great] says: "A law is laid upon the preacher to practice what he preaches." It is useless for a man to flaunt his knowledge of the law if he undermines its teaching by his actions.

But the apostles "spoke as the Spirit gave them the gift of speech." Happy the man whose words issue from the Holy Spirit and not from himself! For some men speak as their own character dictates, but steal the words of others and present them as their own and claim the credit for them. The Lord refers to such men and others like them in Jeremiah: "So, then, I have a quarrel with the prophets that steal my words from each other. I have a quarrel with the prophets, says the Lord, who have only to move their tongues to utter oracles. I have a quarrel with the prophets who make prophecies out of lying dreams, who recount them and lead my people astray with their lies and their pretensions. I certainly never sent them or commissioned them, and they serve no good purpose for this people, says the Lord."

We should speak, then, as the Holy Spirit gives us the gift of speech. Our humble and sincere request to the Spirit for ourselves should be that we may bring the day of Pentecost to fulfillment, insofar as he infuses us with his grace, by using our bodily senses in a perfect manner and by keeping the commandments. Likewise we shall request that we may be filled with a keen sense of sorrow and with fiery tongues for confessing the faith, so that our deserved reward may be to stand in the blazing splendor of the saints and to look upon the triune God.

First Sunday After Pentecost

"God is love," we read today at the beginning of the Epistle. As love is the chief of all the virtues, we shall treat of it here at some length in a special way....

If God loved us to the point that he gave us his well-beloved Son, by whom he made all things, we too should ourselves love one another. "I give you," he says, "a new commandment, that you love one another."...

We have, says Saint Augustine, four objects of love. The first is above us: it is God. The second is ourselves. The third is round about us: it is our neighbor. The fourth is beneath us: it is our body. The rich man loved his body first and above everything. Of God, of his neighbor, of his soul, he had not a thought; that was why he was damned.

Our body, says Saint Bernard, should be to us like a sick person entrusted to our care. We must refuse it many of the worthless things it wants; on the other hand, we must forcefully compel it to take the helpful remedies repugnant to it. We should treat it not as something belonging to us but as belonging to him who bought it at so high a price, and whom we must glorify in our body. We should love our body in the fourth and last place, not as the goal of our life but as an indispensable instrument of it.

CHAPTER 22

SAINT ALBERT THE GREAT

Albertus Magnus, or Albert the Great, is the fourth of four Doctors of the Church to be called "the Great," the others being Basil and Popes Leo I and Gregory I. Albert, though, was actually called that while he was still living. Such was his reputation for being an expert in every branch of learning. For this reason, too, he has been called "Universal Doctor."

Albert is perhaps most famous as the teacher who influenced Saint Thomas Aquinas and is undoubtedly overshadowed by him. Indeed, the thirteenth century is considered the golden age of Catholic philosophy and theology because it produced four Doctors of the Church — Anthony of Padua, Albert, Thomas and Bonaventure.

Albert was a German, born in the castle of Lauingen on the upper Danube, in Swabia, around the year 1200, although some scholars place his birth in 1206. His father was the Count of Bollstadt, a powerful and wealthy ruler. In 1220 Albert was sent to an uncle in Padua so he could be educated at the University of Padua, a renowned center of the liberal arts at the time. (There is nothing to indicate that Albert ever met Saint Anthony of Padua because Albert had already left Padua before Anthony moved there.)

Albert was influenced by the Dominicans in Padua rather than the Franciscans. In 1222 he heard the sermons of Blessed Jordan of Saxony, the man who succeeded Saint Dominic as head of the Order of Friars Preachers. As a result of those sermons, Jordan was able to write that he had received ten postulants for the order. One of them was Albert. When word got back to Swabia that Albert had become a Dominican postulant, his father was indignant and talked about going to Padua and removing his son by force. The Dominicans discreetly moved Albert to another friary, probably at Cologne, where he finished his ecclesiastical studies and was ordained a priest.

He began his teaching career at Cologne in 1228 and later taught philosophy and theology in several other Dominican colleges in Hildesheim, Freiburg-in-Breslau, Regensburg, and Strasbourg, before returning to Cologne.

In 1245 Albert received orders to go to the University of Paris. One of his students there was Thomas Aquinas and Albert quickly recognized his genius. Albert had come to admire the philosophy of Aristotle, a philosophy that had long been dormant in Europe until it was reintroduced by the

Muslims in areas they controlled. Albert showed that Aristotle's philosophy, when refined and purified, could clarify the truths of supernatural revelation. He was a pioneer in what came to be known as scholastic theology, the foundation on which Thomas was to erect his structure of Catholic thought.

After three years at the University of Paris, during which Albert received his doctor's degree and Thomas his bachelor's, Albert returned to Cologne and took Thomas with him. Albert became regent of the *Studium Generale* and Thomas an assistant professor and prefect of the students. (Thomas returned to Paris two years later.) In 1254 Albert was made provincial of the Dominicans in Germany.

At about that time, the mendicant (begging) orders, the Franciscans and Dominicans, were being attacked, mainly by William of Saint-Amour, as not having a legitimate right to teach in the University of Paris. In 1256, while both Thomas Aquinas and Bonaventure were doing their parts to defend the mendicant orders (as we will see in the following two chapters), Albert traveled to Rome to support them there. His mission was successful because Pope Alexander IV condemned William. When Albert's role in the defense of the mendicant orders came to the attention of the pope, he asked Albert to become master of the sacred palace and his personal theologian, an office instituted by Saint Dominic and always filled by a Dominican.

Albert resigned that office, and the provincialate, prior to the Dominicans' general chapter in 1259. At that meeting he worked closely with Thomas Aquinas and Peter of Tarentaise to draw up the rules and schedules of academic education for the friars. (Peter of Tarentaise later became Pope Innocent V.)

Although both he and other Dominicans wanted Albert to be able to teach and write, Pope Alexander IV appointed him bishop of Regensburg in 1260. After two years, and after Pope Alexander's death and the ascension to the throne by Pope Urban IV, Albert resigned that post and returned to Cologne. This remained his headquarters for the rest of his life, although he was called on to make several journeys on behalf of the Church. In 1263, for example, Pope Urban IV appointed him a papal legate to preach in Germany and Bohemia on behalf of a Crusade to the Holy Land. (This was the Crusade during which Saint Louis of France was to die, although not in battle.)

There followed a long period during which Albert was able to write, and he turned out an amazing number of books on every topic of learning then known: natural science, logic, rhetoric, mathematics, ethics, economics, politics, metaphysics, astronomy, meteorology, chemistry, physics, mineralogy, anthropology, chemistry, biology, zoology, botany, weaving, agriculture, geography, navigation, and, of course, philosophy and theology.

Naturally, seen in the light of modern science, his scientific knowledge would be considered rather primitive. However, it is worth noting that, except for Franciscan Friar Roger Bacon, Albert was basically the only one who seriously investigated some of those areas since the time of the ancient Greeks. Albert saw that there could be no conflict between natural and supernatural truths since all truth came from God. One of his treatises, by the way, proved that the world was round and he even wrote that somewhere out in the Atlantic Ocean there was "another island." It would be more than two centuries before Christopher Columbus was to discover that "island."

Albert also wrote things of a strictly religious or spiritual nature, including a treatise on mysticism that had great influence on German mystics of the fourteenth century, a commentary on the Gospel of Luke, and a treatise on the Blessed Sacrament. He saw the Eucharist as the great sacrament of unity, not only between Christ and the individual, but among all Christians who participate in the sacrament. (An excerpt at the end of this chapter is from Albert's commentary on the Gospel of Luke about the Eucharist.)

He had a great devotion to the Blessed Virgin. One of the stories about him is that, as a youth, he was experiencing difficulties with his studies and prayed to Mary for help. She appeared to him in a vision and promised him that, if he persevered in his studies, no one would surpass him in knowledge. However, she continued, his wisdom and knowledge were gifts from God and he would be deprived of them before his death.

His devotion to Mary was shown in his *Treatise on the Praises of the Blessed Virgin* in which he included this passage: "From Mary we receive the price of our redemption, the waters of purification, bread for our soul's nourishment, a remedy for our recovery, the armor for our defense, and the reward of merit."

Albert's resignation as bishop of Regensburg had been accepted by Pope Urban IV in 1262. That pope died in 1264 and was succeeded by Pope Clement IV, who reigned four years until his death in 1268. After his death, there were bitter divisions among the cardinals who had to elect a new pope. It took them three years to do it and it wasn't accomplished until the civic authorities locked them in the papal palace, removed its roof, and threatened a starvation diet. Finally, in 1271, they elected Tedaldo Visconti, archdeacon of Liege, who became Pope Gregory X.

When elected, the new pope was on a Crusade in the Holy Land — a later Crusade from the one Albert preached in 1263. Before going to Rome for his consecration, Gregory discussed with the

Byzantine Emperor, Michael VIII Palaeologus, the possibility of reuniting the Orthodox and Catholic Churches.

The difficulty of electing a pope, the desire for Church unity, and a new Crusade were uppermost in Pope Gregory's mind when he called a new council, the fourteenth ecumenical council. It is known as the Second Council of Lyons. About 500 bishops attended six sessions from June 18 to July 17, 1274. The pope invited Albert, Thomas Aquinas and Bonaventure to attend. As Albert was on his way to Lyons, France, he learned that Thomas Aquinas had died as he was traveling to Lyons. "The Light of the Church is gone," Albert said about Thomas.

The council agreed to Pope Gregory's proposal that popes from then on be elected in a conclave — behind locked doors. The constitution *Ubi periculum* provided that cardinals must assemble not more than 10 days after the pope's death at the place where he died, must stay together without contact with the outside world, and must be subjected to progressively more austere conditions the longer the electoral process took.

As for east-west Church unity, both Pope Gregory and Byzantine Emperor Michael were anxious to see the two Churches reunited, so the pope invited the emperor to send delegates to the Second Council of Lyons. Those delegates assented to the Roman Creed, including the procession of the Holy Spirit from both the Father and the Son, and the primacy of the pope. It appeared that the split was over. Unfortunately, the reunion of the two Churches didn't last long. The council's decisions were rejected by the clergy and laity throughout the Orthodox world.

After Thomas Aquinas died, there was an effort in 1277 by Bishop Stephen Tempier of Paris and others to discredit his writings as being too broad in their adoption of Aristotelian thought. Since Albert was the one who trained Thomas in Aristotelian philosophy, it fell mainly on his shoulders to defend his philosophy and theology. Although he was about seventy-seven at the time, he hurried to Paris and defended his dead disciple, challenging the university to examine himself about Thomas's teachings. Albert was not completely successful, though, because the University of Paris condemned twelve of Thomas's theses anyway.

In 1278, the words of Mary in the vision Albert had as a youth came true. As he was delivering a lecture, suddenly his memory failed. His wisdom and knowledge left him (perhaps Alzheimer's Disease, unknown in the thirteenth century) and for two years he was deprived of his prodigious mental gifts while his body weakened as well. He died at about the age of eighty on November 15, 1280, peacefully and without illness, while sitting in his chair. He was buried in Cologne.

He was regarded as a saint from the time of

his death and his feast day, November 15, was even on the liturgical calendar. However, strangely, he was never even beatified until 1931 when Pope Pius XI both canonized him and declared him a Doctor of the Church. He did this by means of a "Decretal Letter" instead of the usual ceremony of canonization.

From the Decretal Letter of Canonization, by Pope Pius XI

Saint Albert the Great serves as a model for us in this modern age of ours, which longs so ardently for world peace and which feels so confident that the marvels of scientific inventions will assure it a wonderful future. Albert taught that true peace can be established only on the basis of justice and charity in keeping with the divine laws of the Prince of Peace and in his own time he did much to foster peace and concord among the rulers and people of Christendom.

Science also is conducive to the peace and prosperity of the world, provided it is always subject to right reason and supernatural revelation. However, in trusting only in itself and ignoring the truths of religion, as is only too often the case in the modern world, science can do immeasurably more harm than good. The abandonment of the God of justice and charity leads but to social injustice, economic hardships, and the vicious rivalry between nations that brings only one worse world war after another; and in which science, in the service of Satan rather than of God, supplies the weapons for the annihilation of mankind.

In Albert the Great, there is a marvelous interplay between the rays of human and those of divine knowledge, and these rays shine round about him in resplendent glory. He proves to all that between science and faith, between the true and the good, between knowledge and holiness there is no opposition, but rather the closest union. Thus, just as Saint Jerome did from the desert, so also Albert in his wonderful writings cries out with a loud voice and fully demonstrates that genuine science on the one hand and faith, together with a life lived according to faith on the other, can and should flourish simultaneously in man since supernatural faith bestows most efficaciously upon science its completion and perfection.

From a Commentary on the Gospel of Luke, by Saint Albert the Great

"Do this in remembrance of me." Two things should be noted here. The first is the command that we should use this sacrament, which is indicated when he says: "Do this." The second is that this sacrament commemorates the Lord's going to death for our sake.

"Do this": Certainly he would demand nothing more profitable, nothing more pleasant, nothing more beneficial, nothing more desirable, nothing more similar to eternal life. We will look at each of these qualities separately.

This sacrament is profitable because it grants remission of sins; it is most useful because it bestows the fullness of grace on us in this life. "The Father of spirits instructs us in what is useful for our sanctification." And his sanctification is in Christ's sacrifice, that is, when he offers himself in this sacrament to the Father for our redemption, to us for our use. "I consecrate myself for their sakes. Christ, who through the Holy Spirit offered himself up without blemish to God, will cleanse our consciences from dead works to worship the living God."

Nor can we do anything more pleasant. For what is better than God manifesting his whole sweetness to us? "You gave them bread from heaven, not the fruit of human labor, but a bread endowed with all delight and pleasant to every sense of taste. For this substance of yours revealed your kindness toward your children, and serving the desire of each recipient, it changed to suit each one's taste."

He could not have commanded anything more beneficial, for this sacrament is the fruit of the tree of life. Anyone who receives this sacrament with the devotion of sincere faith will never taste death. "It is a tree of life for those who grasp it, and blessed is he who holds it fast. The man who feeds on me shall live on account of me."

Nor could he have commanded anything more lovable, for this sacrament produces love and union. It is characteristic of the greatest love to give itself as food. "Had not the men of my tent exclaimed: 'Who will feed us with his flesh to satisfy our hunger?'" as if to say: I have loved them and they have loved me so much that I desire to be within them, and they wish to receive me so that they may become my members. There is no more intimate or more natural means for them to be united to me, and I to them.

Nor could he have commanded anything which is more like eternal life. Eternal life flows from this sacrament because God with all sweetness pours himself out upon the blessed.

CHAPTER 23

SAINT THOMAS AQUINAS

Of all the Doctors of the Church, Saint Thomas Aquinas is the only one whose theology was recognized as the Church's official theology. First the Dominican Order officially imposed his writings on all Dominicans in 1278. But more important, Pope Leo XIII issued an encyclical in 1879 in which he commanded all priests and students of theology to study Thomas's writings, and Pope Pius XI issued an encyclical in 1923 in which he reemphasized Thomas's preeminent position among all scholars. For more than half a century, most undergraduates of Catholic universities were taught nothing except Thomas's theology. He remains today the dominant spokesman of the Catholic tradition of reason and divine revelation and one of the greatest intellectual figures in the history of the world.

It was not always thus. Thomas had opposition throughout his life since he was challenging the dominance enjoyed by the theology of Saint Augustine for more than eight centuries. As Augustine had Christianized the teachings of Plato, so Thomas did with the teachings of Aristotle. In doing so, though, Thomas found himself in the middle of two schools of thought, those who wanted to accept everything Aristotle taught and those who rejected his teachings entirely. Even after his death, as we saw in the previous chapter on Saint Albert the Great, parts of Thomas's theology were condemned at the University of Paris in 1277 after Bishop Stephen Tempier of Paris and others claimed that Thomas's writings were too broad in their adoption of Aristotelian thought. The same year the University of Oxford and the archbishop of Canterbury censured some of Thomas's writings. And for a lengthy time after Thomas's death the Franciscan Order had such a disdain for Thomas's theology that they forbade anyone in their Order to teach any of Thomas's doctrines or teachings. But we're getting ahead of ourselves.

He was born at Roccasecca, southern Italy, in 1225, the son of Count Landulf of Aquino, nephew of Emperor Barbarossa, and Theodora, countess of Teano. The famous Benedictine Abbey of Monte Cassino, founded by Saint Benedict, was only a few miles away. The abbot there was a kinsman of the Aquino family, Landulf Sinibaldo. When Thomas was five, he was taken there and entered as an oblate. He lived and received his education in the monastery until 1239 and probably would have remained but that year the troops of Emperor Frederick II ejected the monks and Thomas returned home. He was then sent to the University of Naples where he studied the arts and sciences for five years, focusing particularly on philosophy, grammar, rhetoric, and logic.

In Naples he became attracted to the Order of Preachers, the Dominicans, and, without telling his family, he joined the Order in 1243. When news got back to Roccasecca, his mother was furious. (His father died earlier that year.) It wasn't because he had joined a religious community, but that he had joined a mendicant Order instead of the Benedictines. Indeed, Theodora expected him to become the abbot at Monte Cassino. So Theodora set out for Naples to try to change her son's mind. The Dominican friars, though, hurried Thomas off to their convent of Santa Sabina in Rome. Theodora followed, but when she arrived in Rome she learned that the master general of the Dominicans was taking Thomas to Bologna. Theodora then sent word to Thomas's elder brothers who were serving with the emperor's army in Tuscany, and they managed to intercept the Dominicans near Siena. They ordered Thomas to remove his Dominican habit and, when he refused, they bound him and carried him back to Roccasecca.

Once home his mother and brothers tried to convince him that he should be a Benedictine, more in line with his imperial blood and noble origins. Thomas, though, was convinced that the Benedictines didn't stress the development of the intellect that the Dominicans did, and he remained adamant. His family, therefore, imprisoned him in a small isolated castle at Monte San Giovanni, a few miles from Roccasecca. He remained there for almost two years while his brothers kept pressuring him to renounce the Dominicans. His only regular visitor was a sister, Marotta, who supplied him with books that he requested and those sent by the Dominicans. He spent his imprisonment reading biblical writings, books on Aristotle's philosophy, and, most important, Peter Lombard's *Book of Sentences*, a compilation of the opinions of the Church's leading theologians.

At one point Thomas's brothers sent a prostitute into Thomas's room, hoping to tempt him. As she struck her most alluring pose, Thomas got up from his chair, went to the fireplace, stirred the poker in the flames until it was red hot, and began to approach the prostitute with the poker (some accounts say it was a burning log). She screamed and ran out of the room. Thomas's brothers hurried to see what had happened and Thomas slammed the door in their faces. He then burned a cross on the door with the poker.

Later in life, Thomas revealed to a friend, Reginald of Piperno, what happened next. As he knelt in prayer and asked God for purity, two angels appeared to him and assured him that his prayers had been answered. Ever since then, he told Reginald, he had been free from all temptations against purity.

By this time, news about Thomas's imprisonment had reached the ears of both the pope and the emperor and they were pressuring the Aquino family to end it. Finally, undoubtedly with the approval of her brothers, Marotta took some rope and a laundry basket into Thomas's room, tied the rope around a pillar, had Thomas get in the basket, and then lowered him out a window of the castle into the waiting arms of some Dominicans below.

In was now 1245. The Dominicans first took Thomas to Rome where he met with Pope Innocent IV so the pope could see for himself the man he had heard about. The pope gave him his blessing and said that no one should be allowed to interfere with his vocation. The Dominicans then sent Thomas to the University of Paris, which was under the patronage of King Louis IX, later canonized as Saint Louis.

Thomas was not only at the leading center in the world for theological learning, he also had as his master the acknowledged expert in all knowledge, Albert the Great. It didn't take Albert long to realize that he had an intellectual genius on his hands, although that awareness came slower to some of Thomas's classmates. Because of Thomas's bulky size and slowness of movement, and the fact that he seldom spoke in class, they began to call him "the dumb ox." One of them in particular had pity on Thomas and sat down with him and tried to help him with his studies as if he were a child. In humility, Thomas simply thanked him for explaining things to him.

Albert knew, though, that Thomas was not a "dumb ox." He once told a group of the students, "You call him the dumb ox. I tell you that this dumb ox will bellow so loud that his bellowing will fill the world." As Thomas grew more accustomed to speaking out in debates, it didn't take long for the students to understand how right Albert was.

Thomas had first become exposed to the philosophy of Aristotle while he was at the University of Naples and he studied more of it during his imprisonment. But it was at the University of Paris, under the direction of Albert, that he was instructed thoroughly on the thoughts of the ancient Greek philosopher. Aristotle's works had been largely ignored in most of Europe for centuries. However, thanks in part to the Crusades and increased trade with the East, some of Aristotle's texts were being translated from their original Greek or Arabic.

Thomas and Albert were at the University of Paris from 1245 to 1248, after which they went to Cologne. There Albert became regent of the *Studium Generale* and Thomas an assistant professor and prefect of the students. Thomas was

ordained a priest while he was in Cologne. He then
returned to Paris in 1250 and, while continuing his
own studies at the university, lectured on theology at the Dominican convent of St. Jacques. At
this time, too, he wrote an important commentary
on the *Sentences* of Peter Lombard.

Thomas was preparing himself to receive a
doctorate in theology. So was Bonaventure, a
Franciscan who became a good friend. At this time,
though, controversy broke out around these two
men as some members of the university believed
that the mendicant friars, both Dominicans and
Franciscans, should not be permitted to teach at
the university. The leader of the opposition was
William of Saint-Amour, the dean of theology
masters at the university. His attacks against the
Dominicans and Franciscans over a period of years
centered on Thomas and Bonaventure. He was
successful in convincing Pope Innocent IV to re-
scind some of the privileges granted to the mendicant Orders.

Thomas, Bonaventure and Albert all fought
back, Thomas with the publication of a treatise
called *An Apology for the Religious Orders.* Finally
a new pope, Alexander IV, condemned William,
an action that provoked violence in Paris. King
Louis had to send in a troop of soldiers to protect
the convent of St. Jacques. He then used his
influence to compel the university officials to allow both Thomas and Bonaventure to receive their

degrees. They both received their doctorates on October 23, 1257.

Thomas then filled his days as a busy professor, lecturing to students in the mornings and writing during much of the rest of the day. Among other things, he wrote commentaries on the prophet Isaiah, the Gospel of Matthew, and a treatise on the Trinity. He also began work on one of his most famous works, *Treatise on the Truth of the Catholic Faith Against Unbelievers*, commonly known as *Summa Contra Gentiles*, but he didn't finish it until after he had left Paris.

In the spring of 1259, Thomas received word that Pope Alexander IV wanted him closer to him so he could work for the papacy. Although he might have preferred to remain at the University of Paris, he couldn't refuse a papal summons. He was appointed theological adviser to the papal court. His duties included teaching theology to select students attached to the papal court and to members of the Curia, offering his counsel to the Curia on matters of doctrine and theology, and preaching in many Italian towns.

He remained in Italy for ten years, from 1259 to 1269, through the reigns of Popes Alexander IV (1254-1261), Urban IV (1261-1264), and Clement IV (1265-1268). These popes did not live in Rome, though, because that once-great city had deteriorated so badly. Pope Alexander lived in Anagni, southeast of Rome. When Pope Urban IV was elected, he lived in Viterbo, so the papal court, including Thomas, moved there. Pope Clement IV resided first at Perugia and then at Viterbo.

Besides teaching and preaching, Thomas set to work in earnest on his *Summa Contra Gentiles*, applying Aristotelian logic to Christianity in order to attract Jews and Muslims who had been schooled in Aristotle's philosophy. It was used widely by missionaries among educated Muslims and Jews.

Pope Urban put Thomas to work on other things, too. One was *The Office for the Feast of Corpus Christi*. For this Thomas composed prayers and three hymns, including *Pange Lingua Gloriosi* with its sequence, the *Tantum Ergo*.

Another work done for Pope Urban was *Contra Errores Graecorum (Against the Errors of the Greeks)*, used by the pope to try to convince the Eastern Church to reunite itself with Catholicism. It supported the supremacy of the pope and the procession of the Holy Spirit from both the Father and the Son, arguments that were later used at both the Council of Lyons in 1274 and the Council of Florence in 1439-43.

A third project requested by Pope Urban was Thomas's *Catena Aurea (Golden Chain)*, a collection of writings from the Fathers of the Church that provided a complete commentary on Scripture.

Pope Urban died October 2, 1264 and Pope Clement was not elected until February 5, 1265. The Dominicans took advantage of the time between popes to send Thomas to Rome where he taught at the Dominicans' house of studies. He remained there for two years until Pope Clement recalled him to Viterbo. While in Rome, Thomas continued his writing, including a series of ten disputations on questions that were major sources of disagreement between the Eastern and Western Churches.

But of far more importance, in 1266 Thomas began work on his greatest theological achievement, the *Summa Theologiae* (or *Theologica*) — *Summary of Theology*. Although he never finished it, it is still considered the most profound theological treatise ever written. It has three parts. Part I, finished at Viterbo in 1267, is about God, and it is divided into three subjects: "On those things which pertain to the essence of God," "On the distinctions of Persons in God," and "On the creation of beings by God and the beings so created." Perhaps the most influential component of this part was what came to be known as Thomas's *Quinque Viae*, the Five Ways he used to prove the existence of God.

Part II concerns the advance of rational creatures to God, a manual on moral theology and Christian ethics. It has two main sections: on human acts in general and on human acts in detail, in the virtues and vices. Part III, which was never finished, was about Christ: "On the Incarnation," "On the sacraments," and "On eternal life." In all, the *Summa Theologiae* has 38 treatises, 612 questions, 3,120 articles, and about 10,000 individual objections which Thomas answered.

Pope Clement died in 1268 and it was nearly three years before a new pope, Gregory X, was elected. This was a good time, then, the Dominicans decided, to send Thomas back to Paris and appoint him to their principal chair of theology.

In the ten years Thomas was away from Paris, the controversy over Aristotle's philosophy had become a major crisis. On one side of the controversy were the Averroists, named for an Arab named Averroes who had written commentaries on Aristotle's philosophy. Some of his ideas — such as the belief that God exercised no providence in the world — were contrary to the doctrines of the Church. The Averroists insisted, though, that all of Aristotle's philosophy be accepted, even if it contradicted traditional Christian doctrine. The leader of the Averroists, Siger of Brabant, even used Thomas's writings, which he twisted to serve his own ends. He also challenged Thomas's fundamental claim that faith and reason must proceed to the same conclusion, that there could not be a contradiction between the two.

Those on the other side of the controversy were traditional theologians who followed the theology of Saint Augustine, who had Christianized Platonism, considered the opposite body of thought to Aristotelianism. This school of thought was called Augustinian Spiritualism and was championed by the Franciscans, especially John Peckham, the future archbishop of Canterbury who from 1269 to 1271 held the Franciscan chair of theology at the University of Paris, and Stephen Tempier, bishop of Paris.

Thomas was caught in the middle. First he tried to defeat the Averroists, writing a forceful treatise called *On the Unity of the Intellect Against the Averroists*. His arguments were so persuasive that Bishop Tempier condemned thirteen errors in Siger's writings. Next Thomas turned to the Augustinian Spiritualists and wrote *On the Eternity of the World Against the Whisperers*, defending Aristotelianism with the same force that he had used against the Averroists. Bishop Tempier acknowledged Thomas's arguments in December of 1270 by declaring that Christianized Aristotelianism could be taught again.

In 1272, Charles of Anjou, king of Naples and brother of King Louis IX of France, asked the Dominicans to send Thomas to Naples to open a house of studies there. Obedient to his superiors and probably willing to return to the area of his birth, Thomas selected a place for the new school and began teaching there, while continuing his writings, especially the *Summa Theologiae*. By this time he had finished the first two parts and was started on the third.

Around this time, though, Thomas began to

experience a series of ecstasies that made him more and more distracted from his work. He had always had the temperament of a mystic, spending long hours in prayer and meditation. He had visions during the years he lived at Viterbo and Paris and his superiors noticed that his periods of contemplation were becoming longer. Sometimes his fellow monks witnessed episodes of levitation. Finally on December 6, 1273, while he was saying Mass, Thomas experienced a particularly long ecstasy. Afterward he told Brother Reginald, who was waiting for him to continue work on the *Summa Theologiae*, "I can do no more. Such secrets have been revealed to me that all I have written until now seems to me like straw." He never wrote again despite the pleas of his fellow Dominicans. The *Summa* and other things he had been working on were left unfinished.

Pope Gregory X had convened the fourteenth ecumenical council, the Second Council of Lyons, which was set to open in May of 1274. The main purpose of the council was to try to reunite the Greek and Latin Churches. The pope asked Thomas to attend and to bring his treatise *Against the Errors of the Greeks*. Although feeling exhausted and ill, Thomas set out for Lyons, France. He collapsed on the road and was taken first to the castle of a niece and then to a Cistercian monastery at Fossanova, Italy. He died there on March 7, 1274 at the age of 49.

As already noted, Thomas's death did not stop those who opposed his theology. If anything, it encouraged the opposition because Thomas could no longer defend himself. It seemed for a while that Thomas's thoughts were dividing the Church since the Franciscans were so vehement in their opposition. But this opposition softened in the fourteenth century, especially when the canonization process for Thomas was begun by Pope John XXII in 1316 and virtually ended completely when he was canonized on July 18, 1323 by the same pope. At the Council of Trent in the sixteenth century, the *Summa Theologiae* was laid beside the Sacred Scriptures. In 1567 Pope Pius V declared Thomas a Doctor of the Church. He is known as the Angelic Doctor and the Common Doctor. In 1880, Pope Leo XIII named him patron of Catholic schools, colleges, and universities.

The Church celebrates his feast on January 28.

Excerpts from *Summa Theologiae*, by Saint Thomas Aquinas

THIRD ARTICLE — WHETHER GOD EXISTS

Objection 1. It seems that God does not exist; because if one of two contraries be infinite, the other would be altogether destroyed. But the name *God* means that he is infinite goodness. If, therefore,

God existed, there would be no evil discoverable; but there is evil in the world. Therefore God does not exist.

Objection 2. Further, it is superfluous to suppose that what can be accounted for by a few principles has been produced by many. But it seems that everything we see in the world can be accounted for by other principles, supposing God did not exist. For all natural things can be reduced to one principle, which is nature; and all voluntary things can be reduced to one principle, which is human reason, or will. Therefore there is no need to suppose God's existence.

On the contrary, it is said in the person of God: "I am who am."

I answer that, the existence of God can be proved in five ways.

The first and more manifest way is the argument from motion. It is certain, and evident to our senses, that in the world some things are in motion. Now whatever is moved is moved by another, for nothing can be moved except it is in potentiality to that towards which it is moved; whereas a thing moves inasmuch as it is in act. For motion is nothing else than the reduction of something from potentiality to actuality. But nothing can be reduced from potentiality to actuality, except by something in a state of actuality. Thus that which is actually hot, as fire, makes wood, which is potentially hot, to be actually hot, and thereby moves and changes it. Now it is not possible that the same thing should be at once in actuality and potentiality in the same respect, but only in different respects. For what is actually hot cannot simultaneously be potentially hot; but it is simultaneously potentially cold. It is therefore impossible that in the same respect and in the same way a thing should be both mover and moved, i.e., that it should move itself. Therefore, whatever is moved must be moved by another. If that by which it is moved be itself moved, then this also must needs be moved by another, and that by another again. But this cannot go on to infinity, because then there would be no first mover, and, consequently, no other mover, seeing that subsequent movers move only inasmuch as they are moved by the first mover; as the staff moves only because it is moved by the hand. Therefore it is necessary to arrive at a first mover, moved by no other; and this everyone understands to be God.

The second way is from the nature of efficient causes. In the world of sensible things we find there is an order of efficient causes. There is no case known (neither is it, indeed, possible) in which a thing is found to be the efficient cause of itself; for so it would be prior to itself, which is impossible. Now in efficient causes it is not possible to go on to infinity, because in all efficient causes following in order, the first is the cause of the intermediate cause, and the intermediate is the

cause of the ultimate cause, whether the intermediate cause be several, or one only. Now to take
away the cause is to take away the effect. Therefore, if there be no first cause among efficient
causes, there will be no ultimate, nor any intermediate, cause. But if in efficient causes it is possible to go on to infinity, there will be no first
efficient cause, neither will there be an ultimate
effect, nor any intermediate efficient causes; all of
which is plainly false. Therefore it is necessary to
admit a first efficient cause, to which everyone
gives the name of God.

The third way is taken from possibility and
necessity, and runs thus. We find in nature things
that are possible to be and not to be, since they
are found to be generated, and to be corrupted,
and consequently, it is possible for them to be and
not to be. But it is impossible for these always to
exist, for that which can not-be at some time is
not. Therefore, if everything can not-be, then at
one time there was nothing in existence. Now if
this were true, even now there would be nothing
in existence, because that which does not exist
begins to exist only through something already
existing. Therefore, if at one time nothing was in
existence, it would have been impossible for anything to have begun to exist; and thus even now
nothing would be in existence — which is absurd.
Therefore, not all beings are merely possible, but
there must exist something the existence of which

is necessary. But every necessary thing either has its necessity caused by another, or not. Now it is impossible to go on to infinity in necessary things which have their necessity caused by another, as has been already proved in regard to efficient causes. Therefore we cannot but admit the existence of some being having of itself its own necessity, and not receiving it from another, but rather causing in others their necessity. This all men speak of as God.

The fourth way is taken from the gradation to be found in things. Among beings there are some more and some less good, true, noble, and the like. But *more* and *less* are predicated on different things according as they resemble in their different ways something which is the maximum, as a thing is said to be hotter according as it more nearly resembles that which is hottest; so that there is something which is truest, something best, something noblest, and consequently, something which is most being, for those things that are greatest in truth are greatest in being. Now the maximum in any genus is the cause of all in that genus, as fire, which is the maximum of heat, is the cause of all hot things. Therefore there must also be something which is to all beings the cause of their being, goodness, and every other perfection; and this we call God.

The fifth way is taken from the governance of the world. We see that things which lack knowledge, such as natural bodies, act for an end, and this is evident from their acting always, or nearly always, in the same way, so as to obtain the best result. Hence it is plain that they achieve their end, not fortuitously, but designedly. Now whatever lacks knowledge cannot move towards an end, unless it be directed by a being endowed with knowledge and intelligence; as the arrow is directed by the archer. Therefore some intelligent being exists by whom all natural things are directed to their end; and this being we call God.

Reply to Objection 1. As Augustine says: "Since God is the highest good, he would not allow any evil to exist in his works, unless his omnipotence and goodness were such as to bring good even out of evil." This is part of the infinite goodness of God, that he should allow evil to exist, and out of it produce good.

Reply to Objection 2. Since nature works for a determinate end under the direction of a higher agent, whatever is done by nature must be traced back to God as to its first cause. So likewise whatever is done voluntarily must be traced back to some higher cause other than human reason and will, since these can change and fail; for all things that are changeable and capable of defect must be traced back to an immovable and self-necessary first principle, as has been shown.

QUESTION 6 — THE GOODNESS OF GOD

Objection 1. It seems that goodness does not belong to God. For goodness consists in limit, species and order. But these do not seem to belong to God, since God is vast and not in the order of anything. Therefore goodness does not belong to God.

Objection 2. Further, the good is what all things desire. But all things do not desire God, because all things do not know him; and nothing is desired unless it is known. Therefore goodness does not belong to God.

On the contrary, it is written in *Lamentations:* "The Lord is good to them that hope in him, to the soul that seeks him."

I answer that, goodness belongs pre-eminently to God. For a thing is good according to its desirableness. And everything seeks after its own perfection, and the perfection and form of an effect consist in a certain likeness to its cause, since every cause creates its like. Hence the cause itself is desirable and has the nature of a good. The thing desirable in it is a participation in its likeness. Therefore, since God is the first producing cause of all things, it is plain that the aspect of good and of desirableness belong to him; and hence Dionysius attributes goodness to God as to the first efficient cause, saying that "God is called good as the one by whom all things subsist."

Reply to Objection 1. To have limit, species, and order belongs to the essence of a caused good; but goodness is in God as in its cause; hence it belongs to him to impose limit, species, and order on others; wherefore these three things are in God as in their cause.

Reply to Objection 2. All things, by desiring their own perfection, desire God himself, inasmuch as the perfections of all things are so many approaches to the divine being, as appears from what is said above. Of those beings that desire God, some know him as he is in himself, and this is true of the rational creature; others know some participation in his goodness, and this belongs to sense knowledge; and others have a natural desire, but without knowledge, and are directed to their ends by a higher knower.

From a Lecture on the Feast of Corpus Christi, by Saint Thomas Aquinas

Since it was the will of God's only-begotten Son that men should share in his divinity, he assumed our nature in order that by becoming man he might make men gods. Moreover, when he took our flesh he dedicated the whole of its substance to our salvation. He offered his body to God the Father on the altar of the cross as a sacrifice for our reconciliation. He shed his blood for our ransom and purification, so that we might be redeemed from our wretched state of bondage and cleansed from all sin. But to ensure that the memory of so great a gift would abide with us forever, he left his body as food and his blood as drink for the faithful to consume in the form of bread and wine.

O precious and wonderful banquet, that brings us salvation and contains all sweetness! Could anything be of more intrinsic value? Under the old law it was the flesh of calves and goats that was offered, but here Christ himself, the true God, is set before us as our food. What could be more wonderful than this? No other sacrament has greater healing power; through it sins are purged away, virtues are increased, and the soul is enriched with an abundance of every spiritual gift. It is offered in the Church for the living and the dead, so that what was instituted for the salvation of all may be for the benefit of all. Yet, in the end, no one can fully express the sweetness of this sacrament, in which spiritual delight is tasted at its very source, and in which we renew the memory of that surpassing love for us which Christ revealed in his passion.

In was to impress the vastness of this love more firmly upon the hearts of the faithful that our Lord instituted this sacrament at the Last Supper. As he was on the point of leaving the world to go to the Father, after celebrating the Passover with his disciples, he left it as a perpetual memorial of his passion. It was the fulfillment of ancient figures and the greatest of all his miracles, while for those who were to experience the sorrow of his departure, it was destined to be a unique and abiding consolation.

The *Tantum Ergo*, by Saint Thomas Aquinas

> Down in adoration falling,
> Lo! the sacred Host we hail;
> Lo! o'er ancient forms departing,
> Newer rites of grace prevail;
> Faith for all defects supplying
> Where the feeble senses fail.
>
> To the everlasting Father,
> And the Son who reigns on high.
> With the Holy Spirit proceeding
> Forth from each eternally,
> Be salvation, honor, blessing,
> Might and endless majesty. Amen.

CHAPTER 24

SAINT BONAVENTURE

We have already seen, in the previous two chapters, that Saints Bonaventure and Thomas Aquinas developed a close friendship while they were both at the University of Paris. They always remained close, but they also often disagreed when it came to philosophy and theology, thus proving that not all Doctors of the Church had to adhere to the "party line," so to speak. We will treat their disagreements later in this chapter.

Bonaventure was born Giovanni di Fidanza at Bagnorea, a little town near Viterbo, Italy, in 1221. His father had the same name and his mother was Maria la Ritella. Unfortunately, very little is known about his childhood. However, he himself mentioned once that, when he was four years old, Saint Francis cured him of a mortal illness. From this mention, the legend rose, true or not, that his mother had taken the sick boy to Saint Francis and begged him to cure her son. Francis did so and then said, "*O buona ventura* — Oh, happy meeting." The mother called her son Bonaventura from then on.

We are not even sure when Bonaventure joined the Franciscans. It might have been in 1238, when he was seventeen, or it might have been in 1243. Whenever it was, his superiors recognized his remarkable intellect and sent him to the University of Paris for higher studies in philosophy and theology. There, while Thomas Aquinas was studying under Saint Albert the Great, Bonaventure's master was the learned Franciscan, Alexander of Hales. While Thomas immersed himself in the philosophy of Aristotle, Bonaventure remained in the school of Augustinianism which, in turn, was influenced by Plato.

Bonaventure received his license to teach in 1248 and taught philosophy and theology at the University of Paris from 1248 to 1255. During this time he wrote his *Commentary on the Sentences of Peter Lombard* at the request of his superiors. Lombard's *Book of Sentences*, which contained writings of the Church Fathers and opinions of respected theologians through the ages, had become the standard text for theological study, so Bonaventure was one among many who wrote such commentaries. Thomas Aquinas, for example, also did.

Both Bonaventure and Thomas had that combination of profound learning and mystical piety that most of the Doctors of the Church had. But scholars have noted differences between the two. Thomas is thought to have had a keener mind for philosophical thought and speculation while Bonaventure had a more poetic soul and a lively imagination. Thomas's writings were presented in clear-cut but somewhat dry terminology while Bonaventure wrote literature that both enlightened the mind and inflamed the heart. I'm not sure which biographer said it first, but scholars who compare the two men are fond of saying that in Thomas we behold sublime love of theology but in Bonaventure a sublime theology of love.

In 1255 both Bonaventure and Thomas were the targets of lay professors at the University of Paris who believed that the mendicant friars, both Dominicans and Franciscans, should not be permitted to teach at the university. The leader of the opposition was William of Saint-Amour, the dean of theology masters at the university, who wrote a bitter book against the mendicant Orders called *The Perils of the Last Times*. His attacks against the Dominicans and Franciscans over a period of years centered on Thomas and Bonaventure and he succeeded in having them expelled from the faculty.

Bonaventure, Thomas and Albert all fought back, Bonaventure with the publication of a treatise called *On the Poverty of Christ*. Finally Pope Alexander IV condemned William and the friars were reinstated in their teaching positions at the University of Paris. Bonaventure and Thomas were even given the degree Doctor of Theology, both on the same day, October 23, 1257.

To receive his doctorate, Bonaventure returned to the University of Paris from Italy where earlier that year a General Chapter had elected him minister general, the highest office in the Franciscan Order. He was only thirty-five years old and he retained that office for seventeen years, until shortly before his death.

Bonaventure found his Order torn with dissension. The Order had grown quickly after Saint Francis founded it in 1209 and after its Rule was approved by Pope Honorius III in 1223. That Rule had stipulated both corporate and individual poverty, emphasized both the active and contemplative life, and included the staffing of foreign missions (the first rule to do so). But after Francis's death in 1226, many members of the Order came to believe that the original severity of the Rule was impractical when it came to the matter of poverty. One group, known as the Spirituals, wanted to adhere to the letter of the Rule and the spirit of Saint Francis, while most of the friars favored a more moderate interpretation of the Rule. Not all the friars could live the complete poverty that Saint Francis did.

Bonaventure managed to keep peace between the two groups by holding a middle course. At the next General Chapter, in 1260, he proposed a set of revised constitutions, or interpretations, of the Rule, which were accepted. For this he was called the second founder of the Franciscan Or-

der. The constitutions did not, however, satisfy the
Spirituals, who were to continue to live their rig-
orous lives long after Bonaventure died. (The disagreement continued into the fourteenth century,
when there was a division between the Observants
and Conventuals; into the fifteenth century when
the Council of Constance formally recognized the
split; and into the sixteenth century when the
Observants were officially called the Order of Friars Minor, the Conventuals were called the Order
of Friars Minor Conventual, and a third group was
called the Order of Friars Minor Capuchin.) However, during Bonaventure's life, he managed to
keep relative peace.

The General Chapter of 1260 also commissioned Bonaventure to write the definitive biography of Saint Francis. In order to do that, he visited most of the Franciscan monasteries, listening
to the stories of the older friars. He then secluded
himself at Mount Alverna, as Francis sometimes
did, to do the writing. It is said that, while he was
at Mount Alverna, Thomas Aquinas went to visit
him and found him rapt in a mystic ecstasy. Thomas quietly left the room, saying, "Let us not dis-
turb him. It is fitting that a saint should write the
life of a saint."

Bonaventure presented his life of Saint Francis at the Order's General Chapter in 1263. It was
accepted enthusiastically. At the next General
Chapter in 1266, it was declared the official biog-

raphy of the Order's founder and all previous accounts of his life were ordered destroyed.

Bonaventure did not forget the Second and Third Orders founded by Saint Francis — the Poor Clares and the Secular Franciscans. He wrote *Concerning Perfection of Life* for the Poor Clares and established a Confraternity of the Blessed Virgin Mary for the lay members. One illustrious member of the Third Order was King Louis IX of France, whose personal friendship Bonaventure had known when he was at the University of Paris. At another General Chapter, at Pisa in 1272, Bonaventure instituted a solemn anniversary in honor of King Louis, an event that began the process which led to the king's canonization.

Bonaventure had a great love and devotion to both the Blessed Sacrament and the Blessed Virgin. His devotion to the Eucharist was expressed in his writings. One of the prayers he wrote for thanksgiving after Holy Communion remains today in breviaries. (Prayers written by Saint Thomas Aquinas for both before and after Mass are also in today's breviaries.) As for his devotion to Mary, this was shown when he composed a "Little Office of Our Lady." He is also credited with beginning the custom of ringing bells to designate times to recite the Angelus at sunrise, noon, and sunset.

Neither Bonaventure nor Thomas Aquinas was able to accept, or at least to explain, the doctrine of the Immaculate Conception of Mary — that she was conceived without original sin on her soul. This doctrine was fully developed by another Franciscan, John Duns Scotus, a generation after Bonaventure's death. He used some of the principles developed by Bonaventure to explain the doctrine and these were used by Pope Pius IX when he defined the dogma in 1854.

When Bonaventure was forty-four, Pope Clement IV appointed him archbishop of York, England. But Bonaventure begged so earnestly that he be excused from accepting this office that the pope finally consented and appointed someone else. Clement died in 1268 and the Holy See remained vacant for almost three years. Then it was primarily through Bonaventure's efforts that a man he had known while both were at the University of Paris, Theobald Visconti, was elected pope and took the name Gregory X. In 1273, Pope Gregory appointed Bonaventure cardinal-bishop of Albano and this time Bonaventure felt he couldn't refuse. It is said that, when the legates arrived to tell Bonaventure about this great honor, bringing a cardinal's red hat with them, they found him washing dishes. Since his hands were wet, he told them to hang the hat on a nearby tree branch.

Pope Gregory had been on a Crusade when he learned that he had been elected pope. Before his return to Italy for his consecration he met with the Byzantine Emperor, Michael VIII Palaeologus, and discussed the possibility of reuniting the Orthodox and Catholic Churches. In order to try to bring that about, in 1274 he called a council, the fourteenth ecumenical council, known as the Second Council of Lyons, and he commissioned Bonaventure to draw up the agenda for the council. Both Bonaventure and the pope arrived in Lyons several months before the council convened. It held six sessions between May 7 and July 17. Between the second and third sessions, Bonaventure held his last General Chapter of the Franciscan Order, at which he resigned.

Originally three men later declared Doctors of the Church were going to be present at the council — Albert, Thomas Aquinas, and Bonaventure (but only Bonaventure was a bishop and thus a voting member). However, Thomas died while he was on his way. Bonaventure went on to distinguish himself at the council, meeting with the Greek delegates sent by Emperor Michael, and it appeared that reunion of the Church was going to be effected. The pope even sang a Mass of thanksgiving on the feast of Saints Peter and Paul, June 29. (However, after the Greek delegates returned home the reunion of the Churches was rejected by the clergy and laity of the Greek Church.)

As the council continued its sessions, Pope Gregory and the Fathers of the Council were all shocked on July 15, 1274 to learn that Bonaventure had suddenly become ill and died during the night. He was fifty-three years old. He was canonized by

Pope Sixtus IV in 1482 and declared a Doctor of the Church by Pope Sixtus V on March 14, 1587. He is known as the Seraphic Doctor because he was a Franciscan and Saint Francis once had a vision in which the crucified Christ was borne aloft by Seraphim.

The Church celebrates his feast on July 15.

From a Discourse on the Sacred Heart, by Saint Bonaventure

Take thought now, redeemed man, and consider how great and worthy is he who hangs on the cross for you. His death brings the dead to life, but at his passing heaven and earth are plunged into mourning and hard rocks are split asunder.

It was a divine decree that permitted one of the soldiers to open Christ's sacred side with a lance. This was done so that the Church might be formed from the side of Christ as he slept the sleep of death on the cross, and so that the Scripture might be fulfilled: "They shall look on him whom they pierced." The blood and water which poured out at that moment were the price of our salvation. Flowing from the secret abyss of our Lord's heart as from a fountain, this stream gave the sacraments of the Church the power to confer the life of grace, while for those already living in Christ it became a spring of living water welling up to life everlasting.

Arise, then, beloved of Christ! Imitate the dove "that nests in a hole in the cliff," keeping watch at the entrance "like the sparrow that finds a home." There like the turtledove hide your little ones, the fruit of your chaste love. Press your lips to the fountain, "draw water from the wells of your Savior"; for "this is the spring flowing out of the middle of paradise, dividing into four rivers," inundating devout hearts, watering the whole earth and making it fertile.

Run with eager desire to this source of life and light, all you who are vowed to God's service. Come, whoever you may be, and cry out to him with all the strength of your heart. "O indescribable beauty of the most high God and purest radiance of eternal light! Life that gives all life, light that is the source of every other light, preserving in everlasting splendor the myriad flames that have shone before the throne of your divinity from the dawn of time! Eternal and inaccessible fountain, clear and sweet stream flowing from a hidden spring, unseen by mortal eye! None can fathom your depths nor survey your boundaries, none can measure your breadth, nothing can sully your purity. From you flows 'the river which gladdens the city of God' and makes us cry out with joy and thanksgiving in hymns of praise to you, for we know by our own experience that 'with you is the source of life, and in your light we see light.'"

From the *Psalter of Our Lady*, by Saint Bonaventure

Hail Mary, full of grace, the Lord is with thee; blessed art thou among women, and blessed is the fruit of thy womb.

Hear, O most sweet Virgin Mary, hear things new and wonderful! Hearken, O daughter, and see, and incline your ear! Hear that glorious messenger, Gabriel! Hear what is to be the wonderful mode of your fecundity! Incline your ear to a fruitful consent! Hear what is announced to you as a certainty by God the Father! See in what manner the Son of God is to become Incarnate of you! Incline your ear to the Holy Spirit, who is about to operate within you! Because you have ears to hear, hear!

And in the beginning of your hearing, listen to this unheard-of salutation:

Hail Mary. This name, Mary, is not inserted here by Gabriel, but by the devotion of the faithful, inspired by the Holy Spirit. And the last sentence, "Blessed is the fruit of thy womb," was not uttered by Gabriel in his salutation, but was pronounced by Elizabeth in the spirit of prophecy. Let us each and everyone say, "Hail Mary," O truly gracious and venerable, O truly glorious and admirable salutation! As Bede says: "Inasmuch as it is unheard of in human experience, so much more is it becoming to the dignity of Mary."

In this sweetest of salutations five sweet phrases are set forth, in which are contained five sweet prerogatives of the Virgin. Oh, how sweetly are these praises insinuated! For here is signified how most pure, how most full, how most firm and secure, how most worthy, how most useful was the Blessed Virgin Mary. She was most pure, because of the absence of all fault in her; she was most full and abounding, because of the plenitude of grace in her; she was most firm and secure, because of the Divine Presence within her; she was most worthy, because of the dignity of her person; she was most useful, because of the excellence of her Child.

How pure Mary was because of the absence of all evil in her, is well expressed by the word *Ave*. Rightly is the word *Ave* addressed to her, who was ever entirely immune from the "*vae*" or "woe" of sin. Thus it behooved the Mother of God to be, as Saint Anselm testifies: "It was fitting that the conception of the God-Man should be of a most pure mother, that the purity of the Virgin-Mother, than which, under God, there was none greater, should be hers to whom God had designed to give his only Son, whom he had begotten, equal to himself, from his own heart, that he should so give him to her to be at the same time the Son of God and the Son of Man."

Again, how full of grace was Mary by the abounding plenitude of her gifts is well signified when it is said of her: "Full of grace." And truly full, and ever full, as Saint Anselm testifies, when he most devoutly exclaims: "O woman full and over-full of grace, of whose abundance every creature is revived and refreshed."

Again, how secure and firm was Mary by the Divine Presence is well signified by the words, "The Lord is with thee." Rightly is Mary safe and secure, when the Lord is present with her; for the Lord, God the Father, the Son, and the Holy Spirit, is with her, so that she is in an especial manner most intimately connected with God. Saint Bernard shows this when he says: "Nor is God the Son alone with you, whom you clothe with your flesh; but also God the Holy Spirit, of whom you conceive; and God the Father, who has begotten that which you conceive."

Again, how worthy was Mary, because of the dignity of her person, is well expressed when she is saluted in the words: "Blessed art thou among women!" For it could not be that her person, having been made venerable by such a blessing, was not most worthy. Therefore, Saint Anselm, overcome with amazement, exclaims: "O Blessed and ever Blessed Virgin, by whose blessing every creature is not only blessed by its Creator, but the Creator by the creature!"

Again, how useful was Mary, by the excellence of her Child, is well expressed in the words: "Blessed is the fruit of thy womb!" For she availed to save the world, having brought forth the most excellent and powerful Fruit of salvation. Therefore does the devout Saint Anselm say: "By your fruitfulness, O Lady, the unclean sinner is justified, the condemned sinner is saved, and the exile is recalled. Your Son, O Lady, redeemed the captive world, healed the sick, and raised the dead to life."

You see, therefore, dearly beloved, in what manner Mary, because of her immunity from guilt, is rightly saluted with the *Ave*. Because of the abundance and immensity of her grace, she is rightly saluted as "full of grace"; because of the Divine Presence within her, and her intimacy with our Lord, she is told: "The Lord is with thee"; because of the dignity and reverence of her person, she is rightly saluted as "blessed among women"; because of the excellence and utility of her Child, it is fittingly said to her: "Blessed is the fruit of thy womb."

CHAPTER 25

SAINT CATHERINE OF SIENA

Whenever I read about Saint Catherine of Siena, I'm astonished that this young woman was able to accomplish so much, especially considering the status of women in society and in the Church in the fourteenth century. It would be amazing even in the twenty-first century that popes and civic leaders would pay so much attention to one young woman — and a woman that many thought strange, to say the least.

If ever there was a model combination of mysticism and activism, Catherine was it, although some of her ascetical practices would seem to be more for admiration than emulation. She was born in Siena in 1347, the youngest of twenty-five children of Giacomo and Lapa Benincasa. Her father was a prosperous wool dyer who was able to afford a particularly spacious house. By the time Catherine came along, many of the other children were married and some of them continued to live in the home with their children.

She was only six years old when she had her

first mystic experience. She and a brother were on the way home after visiting a married sister (who didn't continue to live with her parents) when suddenly she stopped. Gazing into the sky, she saw Christ seated in glory with the apostles Peter, Paul, and John. She didn't hear her brother, who didn't see the vision, calling her but when he finally grabbed her hand the vision faded. Catherine decided that she must give her life to serve God.

When Catherine was twelve, her parents were already urging her to pay more attention to her appearance so they could find a suitable husband for her. They ignored her pleas that she would never marry. Finally, rebelling against her parents' wishes, she cut off her long golden-brown hair to make herself less attractive. Her parents reacted by assigning the household's most menial tasks to her, which she performed cheerfully and patiently. Her parents also didn't allow her to be alone since they knew that she craved solitude in order to pray. Years later, Catherine wrote in *The Dialogue* that God had shown her how to build in her soul a private cell where no tribulation could enter.

Eventually Catherine's parents came to realize that all their pressures were ineffective and her father ordered that she be left alone. They gave her a little room, only nine by three feet, in which she could pray by herself. There she began her severe ascetical practices: fasting, scourging herself three times a day with an iron chain, and sleeping on a board. She began to wear a hair shirt but later replaced it with an iron-spiked girdle.

When Catherine was only sixteen, she joined the Sisters of Penitence of St. Dominic as a lay member of the Third Order. She received the black habit of a tertiary, usually granted only to matrons or widows. For the next three years she increased her asceticism, seldom leaving her small cell except to go to the Church of Saint Dominic. She experienced both ecstatic visions and periods of spiritual dryness when she had the most degrading temptations. She later wrote that, during those times she would pray, "Lord, where were you when my heart was so sorely vexed with foul and hateful temptations?" and she heard the reply, "Daughter, I was in your heart, fortifying you by grace." The voice also told her that her period of probation was about over.

On Shrove Tuesday in 1366, when she was barely nineteen, Catherine had a particularly important vision. In it, Mary took her hand and held it up to Christ, who placed a ring on it, making her his bride. From then on, the ring was always visible to Catherine, but not to others. Her betrothal was a signal for her that her years of solitude were over.

Like other Dominican tertiaries, Catherine began to volunteer to serve the poor and sick in Siena's hospitals, choosing to care for those with the most loathsome diseases. There obviously was something about Catherine that attracted others to her because soon a group of people — men and women, priests and laity — gathered around her. She called them her spiritual family and considered them her children given by God to help them in their spiritual journey. They, in turn, called her "Mother," even though most of them were older than she. It is said that she could read their thoughts and sometimes even knew their temptations when they were away from her. Many of her early letters were sent to these people encouraging them as a mother would write to her children.

Public opinion about Catherine was understandably divided at this time. Some people revered her as a saint, but others thought she was a fanatic or a little crazy because of her extreme penitential practices. At one point someone made some sort of charges against her that resulted in her being summoned to Florence to appear before the General Chapter of the Dominicans. Whatever the charges were, Catherine was found innocent. The General Chapter also appointed Raymond of Capua to be her confessor. He later became the master general of the Dominicans and Catherine's biographer.

Plague broke out in Siena after Catherine returned from Florence and she and her followers nursed the victims and sometimes helped them to die peacefully. Some members of her circle, including Father Raymond of Capua, contracted the plague and were cured through her intercession.

Catherine also ministered to those in prison and at least on one occasion walked with a condemned man to the scaffold. His last words were, "Jesus and Catherine."

Soon her reputation for holiness grew to such an extent that three Dominican priests were assigned to hear the confessions of those who were influenced by her to change their lives. She was also constantly called on to mediate disputes, something that she seemed to be able to do successfully.

At that time Pope Gregory XI was trying to raise support for another Crusade to rescue the Holy Land from the Muslims, and Catherine threw herself energetically into that campaign. It was at this time that she began to write to the pope, who was living in Avignon, France.

In 1375, Catherine was invited to visit Pisa, an invitation she happily accepted. After receiving Communion in a small church there, she was gazing at a crucifix when suddenly five bright red rays of light came from it and pierced her hands, feet and side. She had received the stigmata and she suffered considerably from these mystical wounds for the rest of her life. They were visible only to herself while she lived, but were clearly seen after her death.

While she was in Pisa, Catherine learned that

Florence and Perugia had revolted against the Holy See and that other Italian cities had followed. She immediately wrote letters to civic leaders of other cities, especially Pisa, Siena, and Lucca, and prevented them from joining the insurgency. From Avignon, Pope Gregory XI sent Cardinal Robert Geneva with an army to put down the uprising, and he laid Florence under an interdict. Soon the people of Florence were suffering so badly that the city officials sent a delegation to Siena to ask Catherine to mediate with the pope.

Catherine went to Florence. There the city's officials met her at the gate and said that, if she would go to Avignon to meet with the pope, they would place negotiations entirely in her hands and would send their ambassadors to confirm whatever she did there. So Catherine went to Avignon, arriving there on June 18, 1376. Pope Gregory received her and said that he wanted nothing but peace. However, his peace terms were so severe that Florence's ambassadors could not accept them and the ambassadors disclaimed Catherine. Her mission to bring peace was unsuccessful.

However, while she was in Avignon, she accomplished something much more important: She convinced Pope Gregory to return the papacy to Rome. The popes had been in Avignon since 1309, through the pontificates of seven popes. Ever since Catherine began to write to the pope about his Crusade, she had also urged him to return to

Rome. Now it was natural that, as they were meeting face to face, they would discuss that topic. Indeed, Pope Gregory had been ready to return the papacy to Rome but his Curia of French cardinals was adamantly opposed. He had, however, secretly made a vow to return to Rome. Now Catherine reminded him of that vow, which she could not have known about, and the pope took that to be a supernatural sign. He resolved to act on his vow at once and left Avignon on September 13, 1376. Catherine and her friends left the same day.

Returning to Siena, Catherine continued to write to the pope about peace between the Holy See and Florence. The pope asked her to return to Florence once more, and she did so, remaining there for some time. It was a city torn by factions and there were times when her life was in danger. Undaunted, she eventually did bring peace, but it wasn't until after Pope Gregory died in 1378.

Returning to Siena, Catherine dictated the book for which she was declared a Doctor of the Church. It was called *The Dialogue*, a mystical work which consisted of four treatises. Her basic theme in the book is God's incredible love for humanity expressed by his first creating the world and then redeeming it through the passion and death of Christ. Catherine said that this love is symbolized in Christ's precious blood. (Excerpts are included later in this chapter.)

After Pope Gregory XI died in 1378, the conclave to elect his successor was the first to meet in Rome since 1303. The Roman people were so afraid that another French pope would be elected, since the college of cardinals was dominated by Frenchmen, that crowds demonstrated in the streets. The cardinals elected an Italian, who took the name Urban VI. Soon, though, the cardinals decided they had made a mistake. Apparently his unexpected elevation to the papacy upset the balance of his mind and the new pope began to subject the cardinals to violent abuse and uncontrollable tirades. The cardinals met at Anagni and published a declaration that the pope's election was invalid "as having been made, not freely, but under fear" of mob violence. They went on to elect Cardinal Robert Geneva, who took the name Clement VII. Thus began what has been called the Great Western Schism.

There were now two popes, each recognized as legitimate by parts of the Christian world. Urban ruled from Rome and Clement moved to Avignon. Catherine supported Urban and began writing letters to the rulers of France, Spain, Scotland, and Naples, all of whom supported Clement. She also wrote to Pope Urban, both encouraging him to bear up under his trials and warning him to control his temper. Rather than resenting her impertinence, the pope asked Catherine to come to Rome so he could profit from her advice and counsel. Catherine moved to Rome and continued to work on behalf of Pope Urban. (The Great Schism wasn't ended until the Council of Constance from 1414 to 1418, decades after Catherine's death.)

Now, though, the years of punishing her body had taken their toll. On April 21, 1380 she suffered a stroke that left her paralyzed from the waist down. Eight days later, on April 29, she died. She was only thirty-three years old!

She was canonized by Pope Pius II in 1461 and declared a Doctor of the Church by Pope Paul VI in 1970. In 1999 Pope John Paul II declared her, along with two other female saints (Bridget of Sweden and Teresa Benedicta of the Cross [Edith Stein]) one of the six patrons of Europe. (The other three are men: Benedict, Cyril and Methodius.) The Church celebrates the feast of St. Catherine of Siena on April 29.

From a Letter to Pope Gregory XI, by Saint Catherine of Siena

In the name of Jesus Christ crucified and of sweet Mary:

Most holy and most reverend my father in Christ Jesus: I, Catherine, your poor unworthy daughter, servant and slave of the servants of Christ, write to you in his precious blood, with desire to see you a good shepherd. For I reflect, sweet my father, that the wolf is carrying away your sheep, and there is no one found to succor them. So I hasten to you, our father and our shepherd, begging you on behalf of Christ crucified to learn from him, who with such fire of love gave himself to the shameful death of the most holy cross, how to rescue that lost sheep, the human race, from the hands of the demons; because through man's rebellion against God they were holding him for their own possession....

Holiest sweet father of mine, I see no other way for us and no other aid to winning back your sheep, which have left the fold of Holy Church in rebellion, not obedient nor submissive to you, their father. I pray you, therefore, in the name of Christ crucified, and I will that you do me this grace, to overcome their malice with your benignity. Yours we are, father! I know and realize that they all feel that they have done wrong; but although they have no excuse for their crimes, nevertheless it seemed to them that they could not do differently, because of the many sufferings and injustices and iniquitous things they have endured from bad shepherds and governors. For they have breathed the stench of the lives of many rulers whom you know yourself to be incarnate demons, and fallen into terrible fears, so that they did like Pilate, who not to lose his authority killed Christ; so did they, for not to lose their state, they maltreated you. I ask you then, father, to show them mercy. Do not regard the ignorance and pride of your sons, but with the food of love and your benignity inflict such mild discipline and benign reproof as shall satisfy Your Holiness and restore peace to us miserable children who have done wrong.

I tell you, sweet Christ on earth, on behalf of Christ in heaven, that if you do this, without strife or tempest, they will all come grieving for the wrong they have done, and lay their heads on your bosom. Then you will rejoice, and we shall rejoice, because by love you have restored the sheep to the fold of Holy Church....

Come, come, and resist no more the will of God that calls you; the hungry sheep await your coming to hold and possess the place of your predecessor and Champion, Apostle Peter. For you, as the Vicar of Christ, should abide in your own place. Come, then, come, and delay no more; and comfort you, and fear not anything that might happen, since God will be with you.

I ask humbly your benediction for me and all my sons; and I beg you to pardon my presumption. Remain in the holy and sweet grace of God — Sweet Jesus, Jesus Love.

Excerpts from *The Dialogue*, by Saint Catherine of Siena

Eternal God, eternal Trinity, you have made the blood of Christ so precious through his sharing in your divine nature. You are a mystery as deep as the sea; the more I search, the more I find, and the more I find the more I search for you. But I can never be satisfied; what I receive will ever leave me desiring more. When you fill my soul I have an even greater hunger, and I grow more famished for your light. I desire above all to see you, the true light, as you really are.

I have tasted and seen the depth of your mystery and the beauty of your creation with the light of my understanding. I have clothed myself with your likeness and have seen what I shall be. Eternal Father, you have given me a share in your power and the wisdom that Christ claims as his own, and your Holy Spirit has given me the desire to love you. You are my Creator, eternal Trinity, and I am your creature. You have made of me a new creation in the blood of your Son, and I know that you are moved with love at the beauty of your creation, for you have enlightened me.

Eternal Trinity, Godhead, mystery deep as the sea, you could give me no greater gift than the gift of yourself. For you are a fire ever burning and never consumed, which itself consumes all the selfish love that fills my being. Yes, you are a fire that takes away the coldness, illuminates the mind with its light, and causes me to know your truth. By this light, reflected as it were in a mirror, I recognize that you are the highest good, one we can neither comprehend nor fathom. And I know that you are beauty and wisdom itself. The food of angels, you gave yourself to man in the fire of your love.

You are the garment which covers our nakedness, and in our hunger you are a satisfying food, for you are sweetness and in you there is no taste of bitterness, O triune God!

* * *

With a look of mercy that revealed his indescribable kindness, God the Father spoke to Catherine:

"Beloved daughter, everything I give to man comes from the love and care I have for him. I desire to show my mercy to the whole world and my protective love to all those who want it.

"But in his ignorance man treats himself very cruelly. My care is constant, but he turns my life-giving gifts into a source of death. Yes, I created him with loving care and formed him in my image and likeness. I pondered, and I was moved by the beauty of my creation. I gave him a memory to recall my goodness, for I wanted him to share in my own power. I gave him an intellect to know and understand my will through the wisdom of my Son, for I am the giver of every good gift and I love him with a father's constant love. Through the Holy Spirit I gave him a will to love what he would come to know with his intellect.

"In my loving care I did all this, so that he could know me and perceive my goodness and rejoice to see me forever. But as I have recounted elsewhere, heaven had been closed off because of Adam's disobedience. Immediately after his sin all manner of evil made its advance throughout the world.

"So that I might commute the death consequent upon this disobedience, I attended to you with loving care — out of provident concern I handed over my only-begotten Son to make satisfaction for your needs. I demanded supreme obedience from him so that the human race might be freed of the poison which had infected the entire earth because of Adam's disobedience. With eager love he submitted to a shameful death on the cross and by that death he gave you life, not merely human but divine."

CHAPTER 26

SAINT TERESA OF JESUS (AVILA)

Saint Teresa was a remarkable woman, as the first woman to be declared a Doctor of the Church would have had to be. She was intelligent, practical, contemplative, courageous, imaginative, humble, and any number of other adjectives to describe someone who displayed great sanctity while simultaneously accomplishing a great deal, especially the reformation of the Carmelite Order, during her lifetime.

One of her writings was called simply *Autobiography*. In it she gives this description of her parents while disparaging her own character: "The possession of virtuous parents who lived in the fear of God, together with those favors which I received from his Divine Majesty, might have made me good, if I had not been so very wicked." There is, though, nothing to indicate that she was ever "so very wicked."

She was born March 28, 1515, the third of nine children of Don Alfonso Sanchez de Capeda and Doña Beatriz Davila y Ahumada, who were people of position in Avila, a city of Old Castile. Her father also had three children by a previous marriage. As she grew up, she became fascinated by stories of the saints, especially the martyrs. When she was seven, she and her brother Roderigo decided to run off to Africa where they hoped to be martyred by the infidel Moors. Their uncle found them and returned them to their home. Failing to become martyrs, they decided to be hermits and tried to build little cells from stones they found in the garden.

Teresa was only fourteen when her mother died and this event seemed to trigger a change in Teresa. She wrote in her *Autobiography* that she became enamored with tales of chivalry, and she even tried to write romantic stories. She wrote: "These tales did not fail to cool my good desires, and were the cause of my falling insensibly into other defects. I was so enchanted that I could not be happy without some new tale in my hands. I began to imitate the fashions, to enjoy being well dressed, to take great care of my hands, to use perfumes, and wear all the vain ornaments which my position in the world allowed."

Noticing the change in Teresa, her father sent her to a convent where other young women of her class were being educated. After eighteen months there she became ill with a malignant type of malaria that was to plague her for the rest of her life. Don Alfonso brought her home to recover. Later she stayed with a married sister and then with her uncle Peter. After returning home, she felt herself drawn toward the religious life, an attraction stimulated by her reading the *Letters of Saint Jerome.* When she told her father that she wanted to become a nun, though, he refused to give his consent. Although hating to defy her father, she went secretly to the Carmelite Convent of the Incarnation just outside Avila and asked for admittance. She was twenty years old.

A year later, her father now resigned to Teresa's life as a nun, she made her profession of vows. But then she had a recurrence of her illness, more severe than before, and her father had her removed from the convent. Several times doctors gave up on her but then she gradually began to improve, helped by a little book given to her by her uncle Peter called *Third Spiritual Alphabet.* It dealt with "prayers of recollection and quiet." Using this book as her guide, Teresa began to concentrate on mental prayer, her first step toward becoming a contemplative.

After three years she was able to return to the convent. Carmelite convents in those days had become lax in their discipline and it was common for the young nuns to visit freely with their friends in the parlor. Teresa began to spend much of her time there and even gave up her habit of mental prayer. In *Autobiography* she castigated herself for "this excuse of bodily weakness" which caused her to "abandon so good a thing, which required no physical strength, but only love and habit."

When she finally stopped what she considered her excessive socializing she found that she was able to once again pray the "prayer of quiet" and the "prayer of union" — meditation and contemplation. She also began to have intellectual visions and hear inner voices, which she thought came from God. However, when she reported them to a priest, Father Gaspar Daza, he told her that she was deluded because such divine favors were not consistent with a life as full of imperfections as hers was.

Teresa consulted with members of the newly formed Society of Jesus. One Jesuit priest assured her that she experienced divine graces but warned her that she had failed to lay the foundations for a true spiritual life by practices of mortification. Another priest, Jesuit Father Balthasar Alvarez, who became her adviser for three years, encouraged her to beg God to direct her to what was most pleasing to him.

During all this time, those who heard about her visions ridiculed her as a victim of delusion or as a hypocrite. In 1557 Saint Peter of Alcantara came to the convent and, after meeting with Teresa, said that he found in her unmistakable evidence of the Holy Spirit. He expressed compassion for what she endured from slander and predicted that she would have more trials in the future. Meanwhile, her mystical experiences continued and she was sometimes lifted from the ground, an experience other saints have known. Later she was to write about her mystical marriage to Christ and the piercing of her heart.

One day, when Teresa had been a nun for 25 years, another nun lamented the laxity of the discipline in the convent and talked about the possibility of founding a new and stricter community. Teresa determined to undertake such an establishment herself and received permission from her superiors. A married sister and her husband built a small convent at Avila in 1561 to shelter the new community. Although there was strong opposition from most of the nuns in the Incarnation Convent, Teresa forged ahead and quietly opened the Convent of Saint Joseph. In 1562 four novices took the habit.

Teresa was now known simply as Teresa of Jesus, mother of the reform of Carmel. The nuns were strictly cloistered under a rule of poverty and almost complete silence. They wore habits of coarse serge and sandals instead of shoes, and for this reason were called the "discalced" or shoeless Carmelites.

For five peaceful years Teresa trained her sisters in religious observances. In 1567 she founded a second convent, and then a third, fourth and fifth. Before her death, she was to found seventeen convents in various parts of Spain and Portugal. This was a remarkable accomplishment considering the difficulties of travel in those days — in mule-drawn carriage or cart on extremely poor roads over mountains, across rivers, and through arid plateaus. Teresa and the nun who accompanied her endured all the rigors of a harsh climate as well as the discomfort of rude lodgings and scanty food.

When Teresa's success at founding reformed communities for women became widely known, men wanted the same things. In 1568, under the authority given her by the prior general, Teresa established a reformed house for men at Durelo, and in 1569 a second one at Pastrana, both on a pattern of extreme poverty and austerity. She left to John of the Cross, who at the time was in his twenties, the direction of these and other reformed communities that might be started for men, as we will see in our next chapter.

While she was founding new communities, Teresa also was writing her literary works. She composed *The Way of Perfection* for the special guidance of her nuns and the *Foundations* for their further edification, but she seems to have meant *The Interior Castle* for all Catholics. In it she wrote with authority about the spiritual life. It is one of the masterpieces of mystical theology.

Teresa's health was poor most of her life, but particularly during the last two years. Yet she still managed to found three more convents. She died while visiting the convent at Alva de Tormez on the evening of October 4, 1582. The next day, as it happened, the new Gregorian calendar came into use. The readjustment made it necessary to drop ten days, so October 5 was counted as October 15, and this latter date became Teresa's feast day. She was canonized by Pope Gregory XV in 1622 and named a Doctor of the Church by Pope Paul VI in 1970.

A Prayer by Saint Teresa of Jesus

If, Lord, thy love for me is strong
As this which binds me unto thee,
What holds me from thee, Lord, so long,
What holds thee, Lord, so long from me?

O soul, what then desirest thou?
— Lord, I would see, who thus choose thee.
What fears can yet assail thee now?
— All that I fear is to lose thee.

Love's whole possession I entreat,
Lord, make my soul thine own abode,
And I will build a nest so sweet
It may not be too poor for God.

O soul in God hidden from sin,
What more desires for thee remain,
Save but to love, and love again,
And all on flame with love within,
Love on, and turn to love again?

From *The Way of Perfection,* by Saint Teresa of Jesus

When asking a favor of some person of importance, would anyone be so ill-mannered and thoughtless as not first to consider how best to address him in order to make a good impression and give him no cause for offense? Surely he would think over his petition carefully and his reason for making it, especially if it were for something specific and important as our good Jesus tells us our petitions should be. It seems to me that this point deserves serious attention. My Lord, could you not have included all in one word by saying: "Father give us whatever is good for us"? After all, to one who understands everything so perfectly, what need is there to say more?

O Eternal Wisdom, between you and your Father that was enough; that was how you prayed in the garden. You expressed your desire and fear but surrendered yourself to his will. But as for us, my Lord, you know that we are less submissive to the will of your Father and need to mention each thing separately in order to stop and think whether it would be good for us, and otherwise not ask for it. The gift our Lord intends for us may be by far the best, but if it is not what we wanted we are quite capable of flinging it back in his face. That is the kind of people we are; ready cash is the only wealth we understand.

Therefore, the good Jesus bids us repeat these words, this prayer for his kingdom to come in us: "Hallowed be your name, your kingdom come." See how wise our Master is! But what do we mean when we pray for this kingdom? That is what I am going to consider now, for it is important that we should understand it. Our good Jesus placed these two petitions side by side because he realized that in our inadequacy we could never fittingly hallow, praise, exalt or glorify this holy name of the eternal Father unless he enabled us to do so by giving us his kingdom here on earth. But since we must know what we are asking for and how important it is to pray for it without ceasing and to do everything in our power to please him who is to give it to us, I should now like to give you my own thoughts on the matter.

Of the many joys that are found in the kingdom of heaven, the greatest seems to me to be the sense of tranquillity and well-being that we shall experience when we are free from all concern for earthly things. Glad because others are glad and for ever at peace, we shall have the deep satisfaction of seeing that by all creatures the Lord is honored and praised, and his name blessed. No one ever offends him, for there everyone loves him. Loving him is the soul's one concern. Indeed it cannot help but love him, for it knows him. Here below our love must fall short of that perfection and constancy, but even so how different it would

be, how much more like that of heaven, if we really knew our Lord!

Excerpts from *The Interior Castle*,
by Saint Teresa of Jesus

This body has one fault, that the more people
pamper it, the more its wants are made known. It
is strange how much it likes to be indulged. How
well it finds some good pretext to deceive the poor
soul! Oh, you who are free from the great troubles
of the world, learn to suffer a little for the love of
God without everyone's knowing it!...

And remember our holy fathers of past times
and holy hermits whose lives we try to imitate;
what pains they endured, what loneliness, what
cold, what hunger, what burning suns, without
having anyone to complain to except God. Do you
think that they were of iron? No, they were as much
flesh as we are; and as soon as we begin, daughters, to conquer this little carcass, it will not bother
us so much. If you don't make up your mind to
swallow, once and for all, death and loss of health,
you will never do anything....

God deliver us from anybody who wishes to
serve him and thinks about her own dignity and
fears to be disgraced. No poison in the world so
slays perfection as these things do....

There are persons, it seems, who are ready

to ask God for favors as a matter of justice. A fine sort of humility! Hence he who knows all does well in giving it to them hardly ever; he sees plainly they are not fit to drink the chalice....

Sometimes the Devil proposes to us great desires, so that we shall not put our hand to what we have to do, and serve our Lord in possible things, but stay content with having desired impossible ones. Granting that you can help much by prayer, don't try to benefit all the world, but those who are in your company, and so the work will be better for you are much bounden to them....

In short, what I would conclude with is that we must not build towers without foundations; the Lord does not look so much to the grandeur of our works as to the love with which they are done; and if we do all we can, his Majesty will see to it that we are able to do more and more every day, if we do not then grow weary, and during the little time that this life lasts — and perhaps it will be shorter than each one thinks — we offer to Christ, inwardly and outwardly, what sacrifice we can, for his Majesty will join it with the one he made to the Father for us on the Cross, that it may have the value which our will would have merited, even though our works may be small.

From a Work by Saint Teresa of Jesus

If Christ Jesus dwells in a man as his friend and noble leader, that man can endure all things, for Christ helps and strengthens us and never abandons us. He is a true friend. And I clearly see that if we expect to please him and receive an abundance of his graces, God desires that these graces must come to us from the hands of Christ, through his most sacred humanity, in which God takes delight.

Many, many times I have perceived this through experience. The Lord has told it to me. I have definitely seen that we must enter by this gate if we wish his Sovereign Majesty to reveal to us great and hidden mysteries. A person should desire no other path, even if he is at the summit of contemplation; on this road he walks safely. All blessings come to us through our Lord. He will teach us, for in beholding his life we find that he is the best example.

What more do we desire from such a good friend at our side? Unlike our friends in the world, he will never abandon us when we are troubled or distressed. Blessed is the one who truly loves him and always keeps him near. Let us consider the glorious Saint Paul: it seems that no other name fell from his lips than that of Jesus, because the name of Jesus was fixed and embedded in his heart.

Once I had come to understand this truth, I carefully considered the lives of some of the saints, the great contemplatives, and found that they took no other path: Francis, Anthony of Padua, Bernard, Catherine of Siena. A person must walk along this path in freedom, placing himself in God's hands. If God should desire to raise us to the position of one who is an intimate and share his secrets, we ought to accept this gladly.

Whenever we think of Christ we should recall the love that led him to bestow on us so many graces and favors, and also the great love God showed in giving us in Christ a pledge of his love; for love calls for love in return. Let us strive to keep this always before our eyes and to rouse ourselves to love him. For if at some time the Lord should grant us the grace of impressing his love on our hearts, all will become easy for us and we shall accomplish great things quickly and without effort.

CHAPTER 27

SAINT JOHN OF THE CROSS

At first glance, Saint John of the Cross would seem to be an unlikely candidate for a Doctor of the Church. He had relatively little formal education, his writings show very little knowledge of the Fathers of the Church, and he apparently knew nothing about earlier writers on mystical theology. Furthermore, he published nothing during his lifetime and never wrote anything with the idea that it would be published. The only way we have any of his writings is that his manuscripts were gathered up after his death.

Yet John of the Cross is considered today probably the greatest mystical theologian in the history of the Church, known as the Doctor of Mystical Theology. The manuscripts that were published after his death, originally written because Carmelite nuns begged him to help them along the path to mystical prayer, were given the titles *The Ascent of Mount Carmel, The Dark Night of the Soul, The Living Flame of Love,* and *The Spiritual Canticle.* In them John presented the stages of

mystical contemplation through purgation, illumi-
nation, and the transforming union with God.

Pope John Paul II has a particular devotion
to this saint. He studied Spanish as a student in
order to be able to read John's writings, especially
his poetry, in the original. The pope wrote his
doctoral dissertation on Saint John of the Cross and
quotes him frequently, especially in his book *Cross-
ing the Threshold of Hope.*

Thomas Merton wrote of John: "Just as we
can never separate asceticism from mysticism, so
in St. John of the Cross we find darkness and light,
suffering and joy, sacrifice and love united together
so closely that they seem at times to be identified."

John was born Juan de Yepes y Alvarez in
Fontiveros, Castile, Spain, on June 24, 1542, the
youngest of three children. Following his father's
death shortly after John's birth, his mother Catalina
raised her family in poor conditions. When he was
old enough, John was apprenticed to a weaver,
but he had no aptitude for that trade and later
became a servant at the hospital at Medina. The
man in charge of the hospital took a liking to him
and arranged for him to attend the Jesuit school
in Medina.

When he was twenty-one, John entered the
Carmelite monastery at Medina, taking the name
John of Saint Matthias. He had already been leading an austere life and he asked permission to follow the original Carmelite rule, without the miti-

gations that had been approved by various popes. He wanted to remain a lay brother, but the Carmelites insisted that he become a priest, so he studied theology for three years at the University of Salamanca and was ordained a priest in 1567.

It was around this time that Saint Teresa was busy reforming the Carmelite nuns, establishing convents of the "discalced" (shoeless) Carmelites. She heard about John who, at the time, was thinking seriously of leaving the Carmelites to join the Carthusians, a stricter order. But Teresa talked him out of it. Instead, she said, God called him to sanctity in the reformed Carmelite Order. She said that she had received permission to found two reformed houses for men and wanted John to join her. John agreed to do so. Teresa had already found another friar, Antonio del Campo, who also wanted to follow the original rule and it is said that Teresa announced to her sisters that night, "Daughters, we have won a friar and a half!" John, who was less than five feet tall, was the "half."

John, Antonio and a lay brother opened the first monastery of the Discalced Carmelite friars on the first Sunday of Advent in 1568. The first monastery, though, was nothing more than a hut, barely habitable. It was at this time that he assumed the name John of the Cross. His joy knew no bounds as he was able to lead the life of mortification and prayer he had wanted.

Meanwhile, Teresa continued to found other

monasteries of Discalced Carmelite friars. When she founded a monastery at Alcala she made John the rector. When, in 1571, Teresa, under obedience, became prioress of the unreformed Convent of the Incarnation at Avila, she sent for John to be its spiritual director and confessor. He continued in that role until 1577.

During this time, tensions arose between the Calced and the Discalced Carmelites. The old friars looked on Teresa's and John's reformation as a rebellion against their order and they refused to recognize the validity of the Discalced friars. In 1577 the Carmelites' provincial ordered John to return to his original monastery at Medina. However, the apostolic delegate, who was in favor of the reformations, ordered John not to return there, and John obeyed the apostolic delegate.

The Carmelites, therefore, on December 3, 1577, entered the convent at Avila, broke open the door to John's room, and physically carried him away. They took him to Toledo where they tried to force him to abandon the reform. When he refused, they threw him into a cell that measured ten feet by six, with one window so small and high that he had to stand on a stool to see well enough to read his breviary.

This was the time of the Spanish Inquisition. On the orders of Father Jerome Tostado, vicar general of the Carmelites in Spain and a consulter for the Inquisition, John was beaten and scourged publicly; he bore the scars the rest of his life. He was insulted and tortured. Later he was to say, "Do not be surprised if I show a great love of suffering. God gave me a high idea of its value when I was in prison at Toledo." However, rather than be crushed spiritually, John perfected his contemplation and became the mystic-poet he is known for. In the solitude of his imprisonment he wrote his earliest poems.

He was imprisoned for nine months. Then one night, obeying an "interior voice," he made a rope out of two old blankets and his tunic, and managed to climb out of the small window. As he worked his way down his make-shift rope he realized it was too short. After dangling for a while, he jumped. He landed safely in a courtyard. From there he had to scale walls before getting to his freedom. Once free, he walked about a hundred miles to Avila where he was hidden by Teresa's nuns and then taken to the monastery of El Calvario in Andalusia.

In 1579 John became rector of the college at Baeza and in 1581 he was chosen prior of Los Martires, near Granada. Even though he was the male founder of the Discalced Carmelites, he took no part in the negotiations that resulted in the establishment of separate provinces for the Discalced and Calced Carmelites, a separation neither he nor Teresa ever intended.

After Teresa's death in 1582, squabbling arose

among the Discalced Carmelites. Father Jerome Gratian, John's friend and provincial, favored a combination of a certain amount of missionary work along with the contemplative life, but Father Nicola Doria felt that the friars should be strictly cloistered. Father Doria won out and in 1585 the General Chapter elected him superior of the Discalced Carmelites. He made John vicar for Andalusia and John devoted himself to correcting abuses he thought occurred when the friars left their monasteries to preach. This was to have consequences later.

The order was prospering now and in 1588 Father Doria was made vicar general. He divided the one province into six, with a consulter in each; John was one of the consulters. But this division caused discontent, especially among the nuns. At a General Chapter in 1591, John spoke up on behalf of the nuns and the former provincial, Father Gratian. Father Doria had long suspected that John was in league with his opponents, and he now took the opportunity to relieve him of all his offices and send him as a simple friar to the remote friary of La Peñuela. Later he was sent to a monastery at Ubeda, in southern Spain, where the superior was a man John had felt it necessary to correct when he was provincial vicar.

John's health was now suffering and he underwent several operations, but the superior had no pity for him. He forbade anyone to see him and even changed the infirmarian because he had treated John with tenderness. After suffering acutely for nearly three months, John died on December 14, 1591, at age 49.

John would seem to have been defeated during his earthly life, a life characterized by suffering, opposition, and persecution by members of the Order he helped to found. After his death, though, his heroic sanctity was acknowledge by all. Miracles performed through his intercession led to his beatification by Pope Clement X in 1675 and his canonization by Pope Benedict XIII in 1726. He was declared a Doctor of the Church by Pope Pius XI in 1926. His feast is celebrated on December 14.

From *The Ascent of Mount Carmel*, by Saint John of the Cross

The following stanzas include all the doctrine I intend to discuss in this book. They describe the way that leads to the summit of the mount — that high state of perfection we here call union of a soul with God. Since these stanzas will serve as a basis for all I shall say, I want to cite them here in full that the reader may see in them a summary of the doctrine to be expounded.

1. One dark night,
   Fired with love's urgent longings
   — Ah, the sheer grace! —
   I went out unseen,
   My house being now all stilled;

2. In darkness and secure,
   By the secret ladder, disguised,
   — Ah, the sheer grace! —
   In darkness and concealment,
   My house being now all stilled;

3. On that glad night,
   In secret, for no one saw me,
   Nor did I look at anything,
   With no other light or guide
   Than the one that burned in my heart;

4. This guided me
   More surely than the light of noon
   To where he waited for me
   — him I knew so well —
   In a place where no one appeared.

5. O guiding night!
   O night more lovely than the dawn!
   O night that has united
   The lover with his beloved,
   Transforming the beloved in her lover.

6. Upon my flowering breast
   Which I kept wholly for him alone,
   There he lay sleeping,
   And I caressing him
   There in a breeze from the fanning cedars.

7. When the breeze blew from the turret
   Parting his hair,
   He wounded my neck
   With his gentle hand,
   Suspending all my senses.

8. I abandoned and forgot myself
   Laying my face on my beloved;
   All things ceased; I went out from myself,
   Leaving my cares
   Forgotten among the lilies.

From *The Ascent of Mount Carmel,* by Saint John of the Cross

Whoever wishes to come after me, let him deny himself, take up his cross and follow me. He who will save his soul will lose it; but he who loses it for my sake, will gain it.

Oh, that one might show us how to understand, practice and experience what this counsel is which our Savior here gives us concerning the denial of ourselves, so that spiritual persons might see in how different a way they should conduct themselves upon this road from that which many of them think proper! For they believe that any kind of retirement and reformation of life suffices; and others are content with practicing the virtues and continuing in prayer and pursuing mortification; but they attain not to detachment and poverty or denial or spiritual purity (which are all one), which the Lord here commends to us; for they prefer feeding and clothing their natural selves with spiritual feelings and consolations, to stripping themselves of all things, and denying themselves all things, for God's sake. For they think that it suffices to deny themselves worldly things without annihilating and purifying themselves of spiritual attachments.

Wherefore it comes to pass that, when there presents itself to them any of this solid and perfect spirituality, consisting in the annihilation of all sweetness in God, in aridity, distaste and trial, which is the true spiritual cross, and the detachment of the spiritual poverty of Christ, they flee from it as from death, and seek only sweetness and delectable communion with God.

This is not self-denial and detachment of spirit, but spiritual gluttony. Herein they become spiritually enemies of the cross of Christ; for true spirituality seeks for God's sake that which is distasteful rather than that which is delectable; and inclines itself rather to suffering than to consolation; and desires to go without all blessings for God's sake rather than to possess them; and to endure aridities and afflictions rather than to enjoy sweet communications, knowing that this is to follow Christ and to deny oneself, and that the other is perchance to seek oneself in God, which is clean contrary to love. For to seek oneself in

God is to seek the favors and refreshments of God; but to seek God in oneself is not only to desire to be without both of these for God's sake, but to incline oneself to choose, for Christ's sake, all that is most distasteful, whether as to God or as to the world; and this is love of God....

I would, then, that I could convince spiritual persons that this road to God consists not in a multiplicity of meditations nor in ways or methods of such, nor in consolations, although these things may in their own way be necessary to beginners; but that it consists only in the one thing that is needful, which is the ability to deny oneself truly, according to that which is without and to that which is within, giving oneself up to suffering for Christ's sake, and to total annihilation.

From *The Dark Night of the Soul,* by Saint John of the Cross

ONE DARK NIGHT

Souls begin to enter this dark night when God, gradually drawing them out of the state of beginners (those who practice meditation on the spiritual road), begins to place them in the state of proficients (those who are already contemplatives) so that by passing through this state they might reach that of the perfect, which is the divine union of the soul with God.

We should first mention here some characteristics of beginners for the sake of a better explanation and understanding of the nature of this night and of God's motive for placing the soul in it. Although our treatment of these things will be as brief as possible, beginners will be helped by it to understand the feebleness of their state and take courage and desire that God place them in this night where the soul is strengthened in virtue and fortified for the inestimable delights of the love of God. And, although we shall be delayed for a moment, it will be for no longer than our discussion of this dark night requires.

It should be known, then, that God nurtures and caresses the soul, after it has been resolutely converted to his service, like a loving mother who warms her child with the heat of her bosom, nurses it with good milk and tender food, and carries and caresses it in her arms. But as the child grows older, the mother withholds her caresses and hides her tender love; she rubs bitter aloes on her sweet breast and sets the child down from her arms, letting it walk on its own feet so that it may put aside the habits of childhood and grow accustomed to greater and more important things. The grace of God acts just as a loving mother by re-engendering in the soul new enthusiasm and fervor in the service of God. With no effort on the soul's part, this grace causes it to taste sweet and delectable milk and to experience intense satisfaction in the performance of spiritual exercises, because God is handing the breast of his tender love to the soul, just as if it were a delicate child.

The soul finds its joy, therefore, in spending lengthy periods at prayer, perhaps even entire nights; its penances are pleasures; its fasts, happiness; and the sacraments and spiritual conversations are its consolations. Although spiritual persons do practice these exercises with great profit and persistence and are very careful about them, they conduct themselves, spiritually speaking, in a very weak and imperfect manner. Since their motivation in their spiritual works and exercises is the consolation and satisfaction they experience in them, and since they have not been conditioned by the arduous struggle of practicing virtue, they possess many faults and imperfections in the discharge of their spiritual activities. For, assuredly, peoples' actions are in direct conformity to the habit of perfection they have acquired, and since these persons have not had time to acquire those firm habits, their work must of necessity be feeble, like that of weak children.

For a clearer understanding of this and of how imperfect beginners truly are, insofar as they practice virtue readily because of the satisfaction attached to it, we will describe, using the seven capital vices as our basis, some of the numerous imperfections beginners commit. Thus we will see how very similar are their deeds to those of children. Then the benefits of the dark night will become evident since it cleanses and purifies the soul of all these imperfections.

From *The Spiritual Canticle*, by Saint John of the Cross

Though holy doctors have uncovered many mysteries and wonders, and devout souls have understood them in this earthly condition of ours, yet the greater part still remains to be unfolded by them, and even to be understood by them.

We must then dig deeply in Christ. He is like a rich mine with many pockets containing treasures: however deep we dig we will never find their end or their limit. Indeed, in every pocket new seams of fresh riches are discovered on all sides.

For this reason the apostle Paul said of Christ: "In him are hidden all the treasures of the wisdom and knowledge of God." The soul cannot enter into these treasures, nor attain them, unless it first crosses into and enters the thicket of suffering, enduring interior and exterior labors, and unless it first receives from God very many blessings in the intellect and in the senses, and has undergone long spiritual training.

All these are lesser things, disposing the soul for the lofty sanctuary of the knowledge of the mysteries of Christ: this is the highest wisdom attainable in this life.

Would that men might come at last to see that it is quite impossible to reach the thicket of the riches and wisdom of God except by first entering the thicket of much suffering, in such a way that the soul finds there its consolation and desire. The soul that longs for divine wisdom chooses first, and in truth, to enter the thicket of the cross.

Saint Paul therefore urges the Ephesians "not to grow weary in the midst of tribulations," but to be "rooted and grounded in love, so that they may know with all the saints the breadth, the length, the height and the depth — to know what is beyond knowledge, the love of Christ, so as to be filled with all the fullness of God."

The gate that gives entry into these riches of his wisdom is the cross; because it is a narrow gate, while many seek the joys that can be gained through it, it is given to few to desire to pass through it.

CHAPTER 28

SAINT PETER CANISIUS

On October 31, 1517, Martin Luther nailed his ninety-five theses to the door of All Saints Church in Wittenberg, Germany. Four years later, in 1521, after the Diet of Worms failed to bring reconciliation, Luther formally left the Catholic Church. That same year, in Spain, Ignatius of Loyola was wounded in the leg during battle and began a period of convalescence that would eventually result in the founding of the Society of Jesus (the Jesuits). And in that year, too, May 8, 1521, Peter Canisius was born in the city of Nijmegen, Holland. All these events — in Germany, Spain and Holland — are connected.

Peter was to become the first of two Jesuits to be declared a Doctor of the Church. (The second was Saint Robert Bellarmine; see next chapter.) He was to spend his adult life defending the Catholic Church against Protestantism.

Peter's Dutch name was Petris Kanijs, Canisius being the Latinized form. His father was a wealthy Dutchman, the mayor of Nijmegen. His mother,

Aegidia van Houwenigen, died shortly after his birth and Peter was reared by a step-mother. When he was fifteen, Peter's father sent him to the University of Cologne to study literature and law, expecting him to become a lawyer. Peter received his master of arts degree when he was only nineteen and went on to study law at Louvain.

While he had been at the University of Cologne, though, he had come under the influence of some pious men and he decided he didn't want to be a lawyer; he wanted to devote his life to serving the Church. After being at Louvain a short time, he returned to Cologne to study theology. He also spoiled his father's plans for him to marry a wealthy young lady by taking a vow of celibacy.

Already as a young man Peter realized the importance of publishing good books. While he was only twenty-one, he brought out a book on the works of John Tauler, a Dominican mystic who lived in the fourteenth century. He followed this up with books on the works of two Doctors of the Church, Saints Cyril of Alexandria and Leo the Great.

Meanwhile, Ignatius of Loyola had founded the Jesuits and was elected general of the society in 1541. One of his original six companions, Peter Faber (or Favre), was preaching in Germany and in 1543 Peter Canisius made Ignatius's "Spiritual Exercises" under Peter Faber's guidance. As a result of this retreat, Peter made the decision to become a Jesuit and was received into the Society of Jesus on May 8, 1543. While continuing his studies in Cologne, he opened there the first Jesuit house in Germany. He was ordained to the priesthood in June of 1546.

By this time the Catholic Church had become serious about trying to counter the Protestant Reformation. Catholic leaders finally saw the necessity of reforming the Church from the inside. Pope Paul III convened the Council of Trent, which lasted for eighteen years (1545-1563), but was actually in session for only a bit more than three years. It began in Trent, Italy but was moved to Bologna because of a dispute between the pope and Emperor Charles V; Trent was under the emperor's control while Bologna was controlled by the pope. Peter Canisius attended sessions in 1547 as theological consultant for Cardinal Otto Truchsess, bishop of Augsburg.

Pope Paul III died in 1549 and his successor, Pope Julius III, reconvened the council in Trent in 1551. It continued for a year, until a war broke out and the council was recessed. It wasn't reconvened until Pope Pius IV did it in 1562. Then Peter was present as papal theologian.

In 1548, after Peter had been at the council in both Trent and Bologna, Ignatius called him to Rome and kept him at his side for five months before sending him to teach in Sicily and to open the first Jesuit school known to history. Then he recalled him to Rome for his solemn profession as a Jesuit

— the eighth man to be professed in the society.

About this time, Germany was becoming ever more Lutheran and Pope Paul III received an urgent request from Duke William IV of Bavaria for Catholic professors capable of counteracting the heretical teachings in the universities. The pope asked Ignatius for Jesuits to conduct this mission and Ignatius sent Peter back to Germany to teach at the University of Ingolstadt.

Thus began the work that would lead Pope Leo XIII to call Peter the Second Apostle of Germany — Saint Boniface being the first. Peter taught, preached and wrote at Ingolstadt from 1549 to 1552, at Vienna from 1552 to 1554, at Prague from 1555 to 1556, at Augsburg from 1559 to 1566, and at Innsbruck and Munich from 1571 to 1577. He established Jesuit colleges in Munich, Innsbruck, Augsburg, Vienna, Wurzburg, and Dillingen. His influence was felt throughout the German Empire, even in places where he did not appear personally.

Shortly before Ignatius died in 1556 he appointed Peter provincial superior of the Upper (or southern) German Province of the Society of Jesus, an area that covered Bavaria, Swabia, Austria, Hungary, and Bohemia. He held that post for thirteen years, laying the foundation that permitted the work of the Jesuits to preserve the Catholic faith in those areas.

Peter was also a diplomat. As the confidant of popes, emperors and kings, he was sent by popes to smooth relations between the Holy See and the German states. He participated in all the principal meetings and councils at the time, including the Discussion at Worms in 1557 and the Diet of Augsburg in 1559, in addition to his work at the Council of Trent. On behalf of the Holy See, he persuaded rulers to support more seminaries as well as the extension of the Collegium Germanicum, the German seminary in Rome.

During all this activity, Peter was also writing. The mere listing of his published works takes up thirty pages in the bibliography of Jesuit authors. He not only wrote himself, but he encouraged others to write and he asked the Holy See to subsidize Catholic publishing houses. Besides scholarly works, he wrote prayer books, the lives of the saints, and other devotional reading.

The works for which he is most noted, though, and the principal reason he is a Doctor of the Church, are his catechisms. In 1555 he published *Summa Doctrinae Christianae* (*Summary of Christian Doctrines*) for colleges and universities. It presented Catholic doctrine through two hundred eleven questions and answers. It became the chief writing of the Catholic Reformation, reissued in more than two hundred editions while Peter was still living and in some four hundred editions over the next two hundred years. Until recently, the word *Cansi* was used in Germany as a synonym for "catechism."

Having written his catechism for college students, Peter followed up with a catechism for children (*Catechismus Minimus*) in 1556 and another for high school students (*Parvus Catechismus Catholicorum*) in 1558.

Besides his catechetical and devotional works, Peter wrote two personal books: *Confessions* in 1570 and *Testament* in 1596. They reveal his inner life, the religious motives that inspired all his activities. He wrote about a vision he had received while he was in Saint Peter's Basilica in Rome in 1549. It occurred after he received the apostolic blessing before setting out for Germany. It was a clear call from God to devote himself to the work of the Church in Germany. (See extract at end of this chapter.)

In all of his writings about the Catholic faith, and particularly when he disputed Protestants, Peter refrained from pretending that the Catholic Church was perfect. The sad fact of the abuses of some Church officials was too obvious. Rather he tried to show that the Protestants were not really reforming the Church, but were destroying it. It was the work of the Jesuits to encourage reform within the Church and this was Peter's approach. He always tried a conciliatory tone.

In 1569, after thirteen years as provincial superior, Peter asked to be relieved of these responsibilities so he could concentrate on preaching in the various cities of southern Germany. He also worked on a series of books that were intended as a reply to a strongly anti-Catholic history of Christianity which was then being published by Protestant writers known as the Centuriators of Magdeburg. He continued to give missions and accompanied the new provincial superior on visitations, even filling the post of vice-provincial.

In 1580, though, he and the new provincial superior, Father Hoffaeus, had some kind of a falling out, and Peter was transferred to Fribourg, Switzerland. Fribourg was a Catholic canton wedged between two Protestant neighbors. He lived there the last seventeen years of his life. He founded the Jesuit college of St. Michael, which later became the University of Fribourg, and preached in the German-speaking cities of Switzerland.

In 1591, when he was seventy, Peter suffered a paralyzing stroke. But even that barely slowed him down. For the next seven years he dictated his writings to a secretary. He died in Fribourg on December 21, 1597 at age seventy-six. He was immediately venerated by the people as a saint, but it was more than two centuries before he was beatified by Pope Pius IX in 1864. The reason for the delay seems to have been because of his conciliatory attitude toward Protestants. It was an era when there was tremendous bitterness between Catholics and Protestants and one of Peter's published works was even placed on the Catholic

Church's "Index of Forbidden Books" because of its lenient attitude toward Protestants. Finally, though, in 1925, Peter was both canonized and declared a Doctor of the Church by Pope Pius XI. The Church celebrates his feast on December 21.

From *Testament*, by Saint Peter Canisius

Eternal High Priest, you allowed me in your boundless goodness to commend the fruit and confirmation of that blessing to your apostles, to whom men go on pilgrimage to the Vatican and who there work wonders under your guidance. It was there that I experienced great consolation and the presence of your grace, offered to me through these great intercessors. They too gave their blessings, and confirmed the mission to Germany; they seemed to promise their good will to me as an apostle of that country. You know, Lord, how strongly and how often you committed Germany to my care on that very day: I was to continue to be solicitous for it thereafter; I was to desire to live and die for it.

At length, it was as if you opened to me the heart in your most sacred body: I seemed to see it directly before my eyes. You told me to drink from this fountain, inviting me, that is, to draw the waters of my salvation from your wellsprings, my Savior. I was most eager that streams of faith, hope and love should flow into me from that source. I was thirsting for poverty, chastity, obedience. I asked to be made wholly clean by you, to be clothed by you, to be made resplendent by you.

So, after daring to approach your most loving heart and to plunge my thirst in it, I received a promise from you of a garment made of three parts: these were to cover my soul in its nakedness, and to belong especially to my religious profession. They were peace, love and perseverance. Protected by this garment of salvation, I was confident that I would lack nothing but all would succeed and give you glory.

A Letter from Saint Peter Canisius to Cardinal John Morone

May the peace of Christ be ever unto us, Most Reverend and Illustrious, Lord Patron.

No doubt Your Eminence remembers that, when we met last year in Ratisbon, I showed you a sample and gave you, as it were, a foretaste of our work on Mary. Now that the work, thanks be to God, is completed and has seen the light of day, I cannot but send a copy of it to Your Eminence and humbly offer it as a gift to you, our esteemed patron.

I know how much this Society of ours, in every place but especially in Germany, owes to you, most eminent of cardinals and dean of their sacred college; I know how your great goodness and kindness these many years have made me your debtor; and I know with what exceptional and extraordinary generosity you have continually favored our college at Dilligen, whereby you have fostered and encouraged to the advantage of all Germany the excellent studies that are there so admirably pursued by so many students. We gladly acknowledge and rightly praise these great benefits we have received from you, our gracious Maecenas, and we wholeheartedly pray God Almighty to repay abundantly with both spiritual and everlasting rewards this truly fatherly charity towards us, your needy children.

This work, then, of ours, which we have undertaken for the sake of defending our August Lady, the most holy Virgin, against the attacks of the heretics, we commend as earnestly as we can to Your Eminence, so that, if need be, you may with your authority protect it most faithfully as your ward here in exile. May the Lord Jesus prosper all your endeavors unto the glory of his name and the benefit of his holy Church.

The bearer of this gift to you is a canon of Bamberg and Augsburg. We would like to commend him for his good qualities to Your Eminence in any petition that he may make.

Ingolstadt, 26 November, 1577.
Your servant in Christ Jesus,
Peter Canisius

CHAPTER 29

SAINT ROBERT BELLARMINE

Saint Robert Bellarmine is the second of the two Jesuits to be declared Doctors of the Church. His life overlapped that of Saint Peter Canisius (see previous chapter); Robert was born twenty-one years after Peter and he died twenty-four years after Peter did. Although they were both Jesuits, Peter Canisius was in southern Germany and Switzerland and Robert Bellarmine was in Italy.

Robert Francis Romulus Bellarmine was born on October 4, 1542 at Montepulciano, a small town about twenty-five miles from Siena in Tuscany, Italy. His father was a nobleman, descended from the house of the Bellarmini, and his mother, Cinthia Cervini, was the sister of the man who would become Pope Marcellus II. (He was pope for less than a month, from April 9 until his death on May 1, 1555; Robert Bellarmine was twelve at the time.)

His mother reared Robert in a pious atmosphere and his parents sent him to the Jesuit college which had recently been established in Montepulciano. The example of his teachers inspired Robert to ask for admittance into the Society of Jesus. He was accepted and became a Jesuit on September 20, 1560, when he was not quite eighteen.

It was an interesting, even exciting, time for the Catholic Church. Pope Pius IV had just been elected the previous December and had announced that he would resume the Council of Trent, which had been in recess since 1552. Just as Robert had been the nephew of Pope Marcellus, so also did Pope Pius IV have a talented nephew — Charles Borromeo, who was only four years older than Robert. The council opened in January 1562 and it was mainly because of Charles's efforts that it continued. It nearly broke up several times but Charles kept it together.

Eventually, the council proved to be one of the most successful in the history of the Church. It issued numerous decrees concerning doctrinal matters. It defined the Canon of the Bible, the rule of faith, the nature of justification, grace, faith, original sin and its effects, the seven sacraments, the sacrificial nature of the Mass, the veneration of saints, use of sacred images, belief in purgatory, the doctrine of indulgences, and the jurisdiction of the pope over the whole Church. It initiated many reforms for renewal in the liturgy, the promotion of religious instruction, and the education of the clergy through the foundation of seminaries. It put Sacred Tradition on an equal footing with

Scripture; decreed that a revision of St. Jerome's Latin translation of the Bible, the Vulgate, was to be the official Catholic version of the Bible; and passed legislation regarding Christian marriages.

Peter lived through all this while making his philosophical studies at the Jesuits' Roman College, completing his work in three years. As the council was ending in 1563, Peter began teaching, first in Florence and then in Mondovi in northwest Italy. He began his theological studies in 1566, first at Padua and then at Louvain, Belgium. He was ordained a priest in 1570 by an eminent biblical scholar, Bishop Cornelius Jansenius of Ghent, and remained at Louvain as a professor of theology. He was the first Jesuit to be commissioned by the University of Louvain to give lectures on the *Summa Theologiae* of Saint Thomas Aquinas.

After the Council of Trent was over, Charles Borromeo was consecrated archbishop of Milan. As Robert was beginning to be recognized as one of Europe's leading theologians, Charles tried to get him to go to his diocese — as did other bishops. However, the Jesuits' superior general kept Robert at Louvain until 1576. Then the pope himself, who was Gregory XIII by this time, asked the superior general to transfer Robert to Rome so he would be close to him. Robert took over the newly established Chair of Controversial Theology at the Roman College of the Jesuits, a position he maintained for twelve years, from 1576 to 1588.

He was teaching at the Jesuits' Roman College when he published his masterpiece, the three-volume work *De Controversiis* (*About Controversies*). Of particular importance in this work were sections on the temporal power of the pope — in which he stated that the pope, as head of all Christendom, had indirect authority in secular matters — and arguments against the divine-right-of-kings theory. His arguments actually presented a middle course at the time, so he was denounced as a "regalist" by those who thought he was giving too much power to the state and as a "papalist" by those who thought he was giving too much power to the pope.

One of those who objected to Robert's writings against the divine right of kings was England's King James I. He demanded all his subjects to take an oath that included a repudiation of the pope's claim to the right to depose heretical kings, and he wrote a rebuttal against Robert's views. Two centuries after Robert's death, Thomas Jefferson was to use Robert's arguments about the limited powers of royal rulers when he was composing the Declaration of Independence, although there is no evidence that Jefferson ever read any of Robert's writings.

While Robert was at the Jesuits' Roman College, he was appointed by Pope Sixtus V to a committee charged with preparing the text of the Church's official edition of the Latin Vulgate Bible, as mandated by the Council of Trent. The committee did its work well, but then Pope Sixtus decided to make a rather thorough revision of the committee's work. It was hurried through the presses in 1590 with typographical errors and other mistakes, but prefaced with a letter from the pope declaring it to be the official Latin Vulgate. However, before it could be distributed, Pope Sixtus died. Robert's committee managed to stop the printing so the work of the committee could be restored.

The next pope, Urban VII, lived only twelve days after he was consecrated pope. His successor, Pope Gregory XIV, reigned almost two years but didn't reissue the Bible. Pope Innocent IX lived as pope only two months. Finally, Pope Clement VIII, elected in 1592, released the Bible. Robert wrote the Introduction in which he stated that Sixtus V wanted to have this corrected edition of his Bible published, and Robert has sometimes been criticized for insincerity or untruthfulness in making that statement.

Robert was appointed spiritual director of the students at the Jesuits' Roman College in 1588 and its rector from 1592 to 1594. Among those under his spiritual care was Aloysius Gonzaga, who died there in 1591. Robert had recognized Aloysius's sanctity and became one of the promoters for his beatification.

Robert then served as provincial superior of

the Jesuits' Neapolitan Province from 1594 to 1597, living in Naples.

He returned from Naples to Rome in 1597 when Pope Clement VIII appointed him papal theologian and consulter to the Holy Office, a position he held for five years. During those years, besides giving advice on theological matters, he wrote papers on dogmatic and moral questions that were being debated between Catholics and Protestants at the time. He also emulated Peter Canisius by writing catechisms — his in Italian, Peter's in German. He published his *Little Catechism* in 1597 and a *Larger Catechism* in 1598. Eventually, the *Little Catechism* was reissued about four hundred times over the centuries and was translated into fifty-six different languages.

In 1599 Pope Clement VIII named Robert a cardinal because, as he said, "the Church of God has not his equal in learning." In 1602, though, Cardinal Bellarmine and Pope Clement VIII had a disagreement. It centered on a theological difficulty that had plagued theologians for many years: How could the Church harmonize two contradictory teachings — that humans have free will and can either accept or reject God's grace, and that God's grace is always efficacious and must necessarily achieve its end? The pope wanted to have this question settled once and for all while Robert argued in favor of giving theologians more time to find a satisfactory solution to this problem. Since it was embarrassing to the pope to have his chief theological consultant disagreeing with him, he removed Robert from his position in Rome and appointed him archbishop of Capua, an important see near Naples. (The Church never has officially settled the theological problem of harmonizing humans' free will with God's efficacious grace.)

Robert now undertook the governing of an archdiocese, but only for three years. While in Capua he continued to live a life of simplicity and poverty, the same as he had always done in Rome, while giving most of his revenue to the poor. It is said that he once even used the hangings of his rooms to clothe poor people, remarking, "The walls won't catch cold." He served the poor in other ways, too, including bringing about a division of several large landed estates into smaller farms for the use of the peasants.

Pope Clement VIII died in 1605 and his successor, Pope Leo XI, reigned for only 27 days. After Pope Paul V was elected, he recalled Robert to Rome and again appointed him a member of the Holy Office as well as to various other papal committees. Thus it was that he was a member of the Holy Office when one of history's most famous cases came before it — that of Galileo Galilei.

Galileo was a famed Italian astronomer and mathematician who accepted the Copernican theory of the solar system — that the Earth and other planets revolved around the Sun instead of vice versa. His work in promoting this theory brought him into conflict with the Holy Office in 1616 because the theory seemed to contradict Sacred Scripture. It fell to Robert, on behalf of the Holy Office, to warn Galileo to stop teaching Copernican theories that were not fully established by adequate proof. (Robert was no longer alive in 1633 when Galileo was condemned for continuing to teach the heliocentric system.)

Among the things Robert worked on during the last years of his life was a new text of the Greek New Testament, intended to be the official New Testament for the Greek Catholic Church. For some unknown reason, Pope Paul V never gave his approval to this text and it was never published. Also, toward the end of his life, Robert published several ascetical works, including *The Sighing Dove* and *The Art of Dying Well*.

He did indeed die well, on September 17, 1621, a month short of his seventy-ninth birthday. It was always taken for granted that he would be canonized and, indeed, miracles were wrought through his intercession. His cause for beatification was introduced in 1627 but it was stalled there through the centuries, mainly because Robert had written so strongly that the rights of temporal rulers were limited. The Holy See didn't want to offend the rulers of the so-called Christian states of Europe. It wasn't until 1923 that Pope Pius XI beatified him. Seven years later, on June 29, 1930, the same pope canonized him, and in 1931 issued a decree declaring him to be a Doctor of the Church.

The Church celebrates his feast on September 17.

From *On the Ascent of the Mind to God,* by Saint Robert Bellarmine

Sweet Lord, you are meek and merciful. Who would not give himself wholeheartedly to your service, if he began to taste even a little of your fatherly rule? What command, Lord, do you give your servants? "Take my yoke upon you," you say. And what is this yoke of yours like? "My yoke," you say, "is easy and my burden light." Who would not be glad to bear a yoke that does not press hard but caresses? Who would not be glad for a burden that does not weigh heavy but refreshes? And so you were right to add: "And you will find rest for your souls." And what is this yoke of yours that does not weary, but gives rest? It is, of course, that first and greatest commandment: "You shall love the Lord your God with all your heart." What is easier, sweeter, more pleasant, than to love goodness, beauty and love, the fullness of which you are, O Lord, my God?

Is it not true that you promise those who keep your commandments a reward more desirable than great wealth and sweeter than honey? You promise a most abundant reward, for as your apostle James says: "The Lord has prepared a crown of life for those who love him." What is this crown of life? It is surely a greater good than we can conceive of or desire, as Saint Paul says, quoting Isaiah: "Eye has not seen, ear has not heard, nor has it so much as dawned on man what God has prepared for those who love him."

Truly, then, the recompense is great for those who keep your commandments. That first and greatest commandment helps the man who obeys, not the God who commands. In addition, the other commandments of God perfect the man who obeys them. They provide him with what he needs. They instruct and enlighten him and make him good and blessed. If you are wise, then, know that you have been created for the glory of God and your own eternal salvation. This is your goal; this is the center of your life; this is the treasure of your heart. If you reach this goal, you will find happiness. If you fail to reach it, you will find misery.

May you consider truly good whatever leads to your goal and truly evil whatever makes you fall away from it. Prosperity and adversity, wealth and poverty, health and sickness, honors and humiliations, life and death, in the mind of the wise man, are not to be sought for their own sake, nor avoided for their own sake. But if they contribute to the glory of God and your eternal happiness, then they are good and should be sought. If they detract from this, they are evil and must be avoided.

Saint Robert Bellarmine's Definition of the Catholic Church

The one and true Church is the assembly of men, bound together by the profession of the same sacraments, under the rule of legitimate pastors, and in particular the see of the Vicar of Christ on earth, the Roman Pontiff.

CHAPTER 30

SAINT LAWRENCE
OF BRINDISI

A man who rides a horse into battle at the head of troops isn't exactly the picture we form in our minds when thinking about the Doctors of the Church. That is one of the things Lawrence of Brindisi did during his busy life, as we will see later.

Lawrence was not his baptismal name. He was born Cesare de Rossi on July 22, 1559, at Brindisi, a town in the kingdom of Naples. His education began with the Conventual Franciscans in Brindisi. But his parents died when he was a boy and he was taken in by an uncle who lived in Venice. The uncle sent him to the College of Saint Mark in Venice.

When he was sixteen, he joined the Order of the Friars Minor Capuchin, a branch of the Franciscan Order that had been established forty-six years earlier, in 1528, by Matteo di Bassi Urbino. Di Bassi wanted to promote within the Franciscan Order a return to the simple, or primitive, rule of the original Franciscans. Toward that purpose a rule was written in 1529 that called for members to adhere to strict austerity while enforcing very firmly the traditional idea of poverty. However, this was not the first time that a movement toward more austerity grew in the Order, as we saw in the chapter about Saint Bonaventure, so there was opposition to di Bassi's plans among other Franciscans. Then, in 1541, the third general of the Capuchins became a Protestant. The branch managed to survive this episode, as well as the near suppression of the entire branch, and then began to flourish in the Catholic Reformation that followed the Council of Trent. It became one of the leading voices for reform within the Church.

This, then, had been the history of the Capuchin Franciscans when Cesare joined them in 1575, changing his name to Lawrence. He was sent to the University of Padua for his philosophical and theological studies, and it was there that it became apparent that he had a marvelous gift for languages. Besides his native Italian, he became fluent in Latin, Greek, Hebrew, German, Bohemian, French and Spanish. With his knowledge of Hebrew and Greek, he studied the Bible in its original languages. He also perfected his preaching style and, after his ordination to the priesthood at age twenty-three, began a preaching ministry in Padua, Verona, Vicenza and other cities in northern Italy.

In 1596 the Capuchins called him to Rome to fill the post of definitor general of the Order.

While he was in Rome, Pope Clement VIII asked him to use his knowledge of Hebrew and the Old Testament to preach to the Jews in Italy. He proved successful at converting many Jews, aided by the fact that his fluency in Hebrew led many Jews to believe that he was a Jew who had himself converted to Catholicism.

After preaching in Italy for a time, Lawrence was sent to the German Empire along with Benedict of Urbino (later beatified) to establish the Capuchins in that part of Europe and to oppose Lutheranism. They founded friaries in Prague in the modern Czech Republic, Vienna in Austria, and Gorizia in northern Italy. These later developed into the provinces of Bohemia, Austria and Styria.

It was while he was in Germany that Lawrence led troops into battle. Emperor Rudolf II asked him to secure the help of the various German princes to defend the empire against the Ottoman Turks, who were threatening Hungary. Lawrence was able to recruit an army and he was appointed its chaplain. The generals consulted him before the battle of Szekes-Fehervar in 1601 and he recommended that the imperial army attack. He then gave a rousing address to the troops and rode into battle ahead of them — armed only with a crucifix. He was credited with the victory over the Turks.

However, Lawrence wasn't in the German Empire long. In 1602, he was elected minister general of the Capuchins. He fulfilled his responsibilities with vigor, making visitations to the various provinces. When his first term of office was up in 1605, though, he refused to accept re-election.

Instead, he accepted a mission on behalf of Emperor Rudolf to talk King Philip III of Spain into joining what was called the Catholic League — countries headed by Catholic rulers in opposition to a group of nations headed by Protestant rulers. He was successful in his mission and, while in Madrid, founded a house of Capuchins.

The Holy See, aware of his success at diplomacy, then appointed him its nuncio in Munich at the court of Maximilian of Bavaria. While living in Munich, Lawrence administered two Capuchin provinces while continuing his work of preaching and conversions. He was frequently used as a mediator to settle quarrels between rulers.

Lawrence didn't write any important books as most of the other Doctors of the Church did. He did write commentaries on Genesis and Ezekiel and his other writings on religious polemics fill three volumes. He is most noted, though, for his sermons which, when the Capuchins collected them in 1956, filled eleven volumes. In those sermons, he usually relied on Scripture quotations to illustrate the points he was making. They show a combination of brilliance and human compassion.

Lawrence served as papal nuncio to Bavaria longer than in any other position he held, but, in 1618, he tried to retire. He moved from Munich to the Capuchin friary at Caserta, Italy, hoping to be free of outside distractions. He was worn out and his health had deteriorated.

His hopes were soon dashed, though, when the leading men of Naples came to see him. At the time, Naples was part of the Spanish Empire of Philip III, whom Lawrence had convinced to join the Catholic League. Now, the Neapolitan leaders complained to Lawrence about the perceived tyranny of the Spanish viceroy, the Duke of Osuna, and they asked Lawrence to go to Madrid to straighten the matter out with Philip III. Much against his better judgment, Lawrence was persuaded to go. He even predicted that, if he went, he would never return.

When he arrived in Madrid, Lawrence learned that Philip was in Lisbon; Portugal was then part of the Spanish Empire. So Lawrence continued on to Lisbon, traveling in Spain and Portugal in the heat of the summer. Once he caught up with the king, he used his powers of persuasion on behalf of the Neapolitans. He made his point and the king agreed to recall the Duke of Osuna.

When Lawrence returned to the place where he was lodging, he was completely worn out. He died there, on July 22, 1619, on his sixtieth birthday. He was beatified in 1783 by Pope Pius VI, canonized in 1881 by Pope Leo XIII, and declared a Doctor of the Church in 1959 by Pope John XXIII. The Church celebrates his feast on July 21.

From a Sermon on Preaching, by Saint Lawrence of Brindisi

There is a spiritual life that we share with the angels of heaven and with the divine spirits, for like them we have been formed in the image and likeness of God. The bread that is necessary for living this life is the grace of the Holy Spirit and the love of God. But grace and love are nothing without faith, since without faith it is impossible to please God. And faith is not conceived unless the word of God is preached. "Faith comes through hearing, and what is heard is the word of Christ." The preaching of the word of God, then, is necessary for the spiritual life, just as the planting of seed is necessary for bodily life.

Christ says, "The sower went out to sow his seed." The sower goes out as a herald of justice. On some occasions we read that the herald was God, for example, when with a living voice from heaven he gave the law of justice to a whole people in the desert.

On other occasions, the herald was an angel of the Lord, as when he accused the people of transgressing the divine law at Bochim, in the place of weeping. At this all the sons of Israel, when they heard the angel's address, became sorrowful in their hearts, lifted up their voices, and wept bitterly. Then again, Moses preached the law of the Lord to the whole people on the plains of Moab, as we read in Deuteronomy. Finally, Christ came as God and man to preach the word of the Lord, and for the same purpose he sent the apostles, just as he had sent the prophets before them.

Preaching, therefore, is a duty that is apostolic, angelic, Christian, divine. The word of God is replete with manifold blessings, since it is, so to speak, a treasure of all goods. It is the source of faith, hope, charity, all virtues, all the gifts of the Holy Spirit, all the beatitudes of the Gospel, all good works, all the rewards of life, all the glory of paradise: "Welcome the word that has taken root in you, with its power to save you."

For the word of God is a light to the mind and a fire to the will. It enables man to know God and to love him. And for the interior man who lives by the Spirit of God through grace, it is bread and water, but a bread sweeter than honey and the honeycomb, a water better than wine and milk. For the soul it is a spiritual treasure of merits yielding an abundance of gold and precious stones. Against the hardness of a heart that persists in wrongdoing, it acts as a hammer. Against the world, the flesh and the devil, it serves as a sword that destroys all sin.

From a Sermon by Saint Lawrence of Brindisi

God is love, and all his operations proceed from love. Once he wills to manifest that goodness by sharing his love outside himself, then the Incarnation becomes the supreme manifestation of his goodness and love and glory. So, Christ was intended before all other creatures and for his own sake. For him all things were created and to him all things must be subject, and God loves all creatures in and because of Christ. Christ is the firstborn of every creature, and the whole of humanity as well as the created world finds its foundation and meaning in him. Moreover, this would have been the case even if Adam had not sinned.

CHAPTER 31

SAINT FRANCIS DE SALES

In the history of Christianity, Saint Francis de Sales' *Introduction to the Devout Life* and Thomas à Kempis's *Imitation of Christ* are probably the best and most practical books ever written about individual piety. In his book, Francis emphasized that we are all called to sanctity but that the devotions of lay people who are busy in a secular world must be different from those of priests or religious. But this was only one of the things Francis wrote and only one of the reasons why he is both a Doctor of the Church and the patron of the Catholic press.

He was born on August 21, 1567 at the Chateau de Sales in Swiss Savoy, the eldest of thirteen children. His father was an aristocrat. His mother, who was only fifteen when Francis was born, began to teach him herself. As Francis grew, his mother was helped by the Abbé Deage, who served as his tutor. When he was eight, Francis went, along with Abbé Deage, to the College of Annecy, where he made his first Communion and received confirmation. When he was fourteen,

Francis and Abbé Deage were sent to the University of Paris, one of the great centers of learning. His father wanted him to enroll in the university's College of Navarre because other sons of noblemen attended that college, but Francis preferred the College of Clermont because it was directed by the Jesuits. His father finally consented.

Francis excelled at the College of Clermont in rhetoric and philosophy, but his favorite subjects were theology and Scripture. Under the direction of both Abbé Deage and the Jesuits, his spiritual life matured and he decided he wanted to give his life to God. He placed himself under the special protection of the Blessed Virgin and took a vow of perpetual chastity.

After six years at the University of Paris, Francis's father sent him to the University of Padua where he studied jurisprudence for four years and earned his doctor of law degree at age twenty-four. He then returned to his parents' chateau and, for eighteen months, lived the life of a young nobleman. His father wanted him to settle down and had even selected a bride for him. Furthermore, the prince of Savoy offered him a seat in the senate. Francis annoyed his father by refusing both.

He had decided to become a priest but, up to that time, had confided only in his mother and to a few intimate friends, including his cousin, Canon Louis de Sales. Eventually, though, he had to face his father who, he knew, would be vigorously opposed. Then it happened that the provost of the chapter of cathedral canons in Geneva died. Canon Louis de Sales thought that Francis could be appointed to that position, and, if so, it would help Francis get his father's approval to become a priest. The position was offered, Francis accepted it, and his father reluctantly consented. Francis was so well prepared that his ordination was speeded up; he was ordained a deacon three weeks after his father gave his consent and was ordained a priest six months after that, on December 18, 1593, at age twenty-six.

He undertook his duties as provost of Geneva, but with headquarters in Annecy rather than in Geneva because that city was in Calvinist hands. Switzerland at that time was sharply divided along religious lines, especially in the Chablais, a section of Savoy along the southern shore of Lake Geneva. Protestants from Berne had invaded the area some sixty years earlier and outlawed Catholic worship there. Later, the duke of Savoy regained Chablais but on condition that Catholicism remain forbidden. In 1589 Berne's Protestants again invaded the Chablais, but were repulsed. The Treaty of Nyon that followed that victory allowed for the reestablishment of Catholic worship, limiting Protestant teaching to three towns. But that treaty was soon broken and in 1594 the Protestants once again controlled most of the Chablais.

Thus it was that, soon after Francis's ordination, Bishop Claude de Granier of Geneva sought missionaries to send to Chablais. Francis and his cousin, Louis de Sales, volunteered and the bishop accepted them. They set out for the Chateau des Allinges, six or seven miles from Thonon, the capital of Chablais. The chateau was a Catholic stronghold where the governor had a garrison of soldiers, so the two de Sales cousins had to return there each night for safety. In Thonon the Catholic population was reduced to about twenty people, who were afraid to declare themselves openly, so Francis and Louis had to seek them out and encourage them in their faith. Soon they expanded their efforts to other villages in the surrounding countryside.

It was a difficult life for the two cousins, especially in winter when they had to make that walk to and from Allinges every morning and night in Switzerland's weather. Once wolves attacked Francis and he escaped by spending the night in a tree. When morning came, he was discovered by some peasants and he probably would have died from exposure if they hadn't taken him to their hut and revived him with warmth. On two other occasions, Francis was waylaid by Protestants who had sworn to kill him. Francis's escape both times apparently was miraculous.

At first the missionaries' efforts met with little apparent success. Francis tried every way he could think of to reach the minds and hearts of the people, and it was at this time that he began writing leaflets about Catholic doctrine, comparing it to the teachings of Calvinism. These little papers, laboriously copied by hand and distributed by any means available, were the beginning of Francis's work as a writer. Later they were collected and printed in a volume called *Controversies.*

In 1595, as he was climbing the mountain of Voiron to help restore an oratory to the Blessed Virgin which had been destroyed by the Calvinists, he was attacked by a crowd and beaten. Soon after that, though, his sermons in Thonon began to draw larger crowds, probably because of the little leaflets. Soon there was a stream of lapsed Catholics seeking reconciliation with the Catholic Church, and Francis felt safe enough to leave the Chateau des Allinges and live openly in Thonon. He preached in the marketplace and had public debates with some of the Calvinist leaders in the area.

In 1597 Pope Clement VIII asked Francis to go to Geneva to debate Theodore de Beza, a distinguished Calvinist scholar. Francis was unable to bring Beza back into the Catholic Church, but the debate did bring many others back.

After several years, Bishop de Granier visited the mission and was amazed at the progress Francis and Louis had made. The bishop administered confirmation and even presided at a Forty Hours devotion.

The bishop was considering a successor and approached Francis with the idea of making him coadjutor bishop. At first Francis modestly declined but, as the bishop persisted, came to believe that it was God's will for him, so he agreed. The bishop sent him to Rome to meet with Pope Clement VIII, who would make the appointment. The pope had heard much about this young priest, especially after his debate with Theodore de Beza, and decided to have him examined in his presence. Among those doing the examination were Cardinal Robert Bellarmine and the noted Church historian Cesare Baronius. Thirty-five theological questions were put to Francis and he answered them all with simplicity and modesty but in a way that proved his learning. The pope was more than satisfied and made the appointment. Francis returned to Annecy.

Early in 1602, Bishop de Granier sent Francis to Paris to discuss the French section of the diocese of Geneva with King Henry IV, who had recently asserted his sovereignty over all France. The king was so impressed with Francis that he tried to persuade him to remain in France, but Francis declined. He also was invited to preach a series of sermons in the Chapel Royal at Paris to overflowing crowds.

Bishop de Granier died later in 1602 and Francis, then thirty-five, succeeded to the see of Geneva, with residence still in Annecy. He ran his household according to evangelical poverty and continued to preach and hear confessions. He promoted the teaching of catechism throughout the diocese and he himself gave instructions in Annecy. He also carried on a large correspondence in which he gave sympathetic guidance to many people. He practiced his axiom, "A spoonful of honey attracts more flies than a barrelful of vinegar."

In 1604 Francis met Jeanne Françoise Fremyot, the baroness of Chantal (later known as Saint Jane Frances de Chantal), while he was preaching Lenten sermons in Dijon, France. She told Francis that, three years earlier, her husband had died in a hunting accident when she was only twenty-nine. Now she wanted to enter religious life although she still had three young children. Francis advised her to wait until her children were older before making such a decision, but he continued corresponding with her. After several years passed, he told Jane Frances that he wanted to found an institute of women to meet the needs of widows and lonely women in poor health who were unable to join other religious Orders because of their physical condition. There would be no cloister and the women would be free to perform spiritual and corporate works of mercy.

Francis and Jane Frances founded the Order of the Visitation in 1610. Not all of their plans worked out. Because of opposition to the idea of women in active ministry current at the time, Francis eventually had to make it a cloistered community with the rule of Saint Augustine. He wrote his *Treatise on the Love of God* for the Visitation Sisters in 1616. A famous passage from that work is, "The measure of love is to love without measure."

Francis's book *Introduction to the Devout Life* began as letters that he wrote to Madame de Chamoisy, a cousin by marriage. She showed the letters to a Jesuit priest, Father Jean Fourier, who urged Francis to publish them as a book. Francis worked on the book in 1607 and 1608 and it was published in 1609. It was immediately recognized as a masterpiece of mystical and devotional literature and was translated into many other languages. During the next ten years he made revisions and published four more editions. Perhaps his book can be summed up by a sentence that appears at the end of a paragraph in the thirteenth section of the fourth part of the book: "True devotion consists in a constant, resolute, prompt, and active will to do whatever we know is pleasing to God."

In 1622, the duke of Savoy invited Francis to accompany him on a trip to France to meet with King Louis XIII. Francis accepted, but he seems to have had a premonition that he would not return because he put all his affairs in order before leaving. At Avignon, he preached often. On the return home, he stopped at the Visitation convent at Lyons where he spent a month giving instructions and advice to the Sisters. He stayed there over

Christmas. On December 27, he suffered a paralyzing stroke, but regained consciousness and his speech. He died the following day, December 28, 1622, at age fifty-five.

Francis was beatified by Pope Alexander VII in 1661, the first beatification to be held in Saint Peter's Basilica in the Vatican. He was canonized by the same pope in 1665, was declared a Doctor of the Church by Pope Pius IX in 1877, and named the patron of Catholic writers and the Catholic press by Pope Pius XI in 1923. The Church celebrates his feast on January 24.

Excerpts from *Introduction to the Devout Life*, by Saint Francis de Sales

When God the Creator made all things, he commanded the plants to bring forth fruit each according to its own kind; he has likewise commanded Christians, who are the living plants of his Church, to bring forth the fruits of devotion, each one in accord with his character, his station and his calling.

I say that devotion must be practiced in different ways by the nobleman and by the working man, by the servant and by the prince, by the widow, by the unmarried girl and by the married woman. But even this distinction is not sufficient; for the practice of devotion must be adapted to the strength, to the occupation and to the duties of each one in particular.

Tell me, please, my Philothea, whether it is proper for a bishop to want to lead a solitary life like a Carthusian; or for married people to be no more concerned than a Capuchin about increasing their income; or for a working man to spend his whole day in church like a religious; or on the other hand for a religious to be constantly exposed like a bishop to all the events and circumstances that bear on the needs of our neighbor. Is not this sort of devotion ridiculous, unorganized and intolerable? Yet this absurd error occurs very frequently, but in no way does true devotion, my Philothea, destroy anything at all. On the contrary, it perfects and fulfills all things. In fact if it ever works against, or is inimical to, anyone's legitimate station and calling, then it is very definitely false devotion.

The bee collects honey from flowers in such a way as to do the least damage or destruction to them, and he leaves them whole, undamaged and fresh, just as he found them. True devotion does still better. Not only does it not injure any sort of calling or occupation, it even embellishes and enhances it.

Moreover, just as every sort of gem, cast in honey, becomes brighter and more sparkling, each according to its color, so each person becomes more acceptable and fitting in his own vocation when he sets his vocation in the context of devotion. Through devotion your family cares become more peaceful, mutual love between husband and wife becomes more sincere, the service we owe to the prince becomes more faithful, and our work, no matter what it is, becomes more pleasant and agreeable.

It is therefore an error, and even a heresy, to wish to exclude the exercise of devotion from military divisions, from the artisans' shops, from the courts of princes, from family households. I acknowledge, my dear Philothea, that the type of devotion which is purely contemplative, monastic and religious can certainly not be exercised in these sorts of stations and occupations, but besides this threefold type of devotion, there are many others fit for perfecting those who live in a secular state.

Therefore, in whatever situations we happen to be, we can and we must aspire to the life of perfection.

* * *

To hear Mass in a proper manner, either actually or spiritually:

(1) From the beginning until the priest goes up to the altar make your preparation with him. This consists in placing yourself in the presence of God, recognizing your unworthiness, and asking pardon for your sins.

(2) From the time he goes up to the altar until

the Gospel consider our Lord's coming and his life in this world by a simple, general consideration.

(3) From the Gospel until after the Creed consider our Savior's preaching and affirm that you are resolved to live and die faithful and obedient to his holy word and in union with the holy Catholic Church.

(4) From the Creed to the Our Father apply your heart to the mysteries of the passion and death of our Redeemer. They are actually and essentially represented in this holy Sacrifice. Together with the priest and the rest of the people you will offer them to God the Father for his honor and for your own salvation.

(5) From the Our Father to the Communion strive to excite a thousand desires in your heart and ardently wish to be joined and united forever to our Savior in everlasting love.

(6) From the Communion to the end of Mass give thanks to Jesus Christ for his incarnation, life, passion, and death, and for the love he manifests in his Holy Sacrifice. Implore him always to be merciful to you, your parents, friends, and the whole Church. Humble yourself with all your heart and devoutly receive the blessing our Lord gives you through the ministry of his minister.

If you wish to meditate during Mass on the mysteries you have proposed from day to day, there is no need to change your plan and make all these particular acts. It will suffice that at the beginning you direct your intention to adore and offer this Holy Sacrifice by the exercise of meditation and prayer. In all meditations the aforesaid acts are found either explicitly or implicitly and virtually.

* * *

As soon as you are conscious of being tempted, follow the example of children when they see a wolf or bear out in the country. They immediately run to the arms of their father or mother or at least call to them for help and protection. Turn in the same way to God and implore his mercy and help. This is the remedy our Lord himself has taught us: "Pray that you do not enter into temptation."

If you find that the temptation still continues or even increases, run in spirit to embrace the Holy Cross as if you saw Christ Jesus crucified before you. Insist that you will never consent to the temptation, implore his assistance against it, and continue steadfastly to protest that you will refuse consent as long as the temptation continues. When you make such protestations and refusals of consent, do not look the temptation in the face but look solely at our Lord. If you look at the temptation, especially when it is strong, it may shake your courage.

Turn your thoughts to some good, commendable activity. When such thoughts enter and find place in your heart, they will drive away temptations and evil thoughts.

The sovereign remedy against all temptation, whether great or small, is to open your heart and express its suggestions, feelings, and affections to your director. Note well that the first condition the evil one makes with a soul he desires to seduce is for it to keep silence, just as those who want to seduce girls or women from the very first forbid them to say anything about their proposals to father or husband. On the other hand, in his inspirations God requires that we make the temptations known to our superiors and directors.

If temptation continues to harass and persecute us after all this, there is nothing further to do on our part but to remain steadfast in our protestations never to consent to it. Just as girls can never be married as long as they say no, so too a soul though tempted can never sin as long as it says no.

* * *

Reflect upon the everlasting love God has had for you. Before our Lord Jesus Christ as man suffered on the cross for you his Divine Majesty by his sovereign goodness already foresaw your existence and loved and favored you. When did his love for you begin? It began even when he began to be God. When did he begin to be God? Never, for he has been forever, without beginning and without end. So also he has always loved you from all eternity and for this reason he has prepared for you all these graces and favors.

Hence he speaks to you as well as to others when he says by the prophet, "I have loved you with an everlasting love, therefore have I drawn you, taking pity on you." Among other things, he has thought of enabling you to make your resolution to serve him.

O God, what resolutions are these which you have thought of and meditated upon and projected from all eternity! How dear and precious should they be to us! What should we not suffer rather than forget the least of them! Rather let the whole world perish! For all the world together is not worth one single soul and a soul is worth nothing without these resolutions.

CHAPTER 32

SAINT ALPHONSUS
DE LIGUORI

Saint Alphonsus de Liguori was probably the greatest moral theologian in the history of the Catholic Church. He is considered, in fact, the "father" of moral theology since he, more than anyone else, made it a separate ecclesiastical science rather than only a secondary branch of theology in general. He steered a middle course between the extremes of moral laxity and the rigorism of Jansenism of the eighteenth century.

His masterpiece, *Theologiae Moralis* (*Moral Theology*) went through sixty editions during the century after it was written, nine during his lifetime. In this work, he assembled seventy thousand quotations from the Fathers and Doctors of the Church, and other earlier theologians. He achieved such renown that the Holy See, in a decree dated July 22, 1831, declared that priests could follow any opinion of Saint Alphonsus on moral questions.

Alphonsus became such a great moral theologian while leading an active life that included the founding of a religious Order, preaching missions, and serving as a bishop for a time. He also wrote more than a hundred other books and pamphlets besides *Moral Theology*. He also experienced more than his share of tragedy.

Born on September 27, 1696, he was the eldest of eight children of Don Joseph de Liguori, a captain in the royal navy of the Kingdom of Naples, and Doña Anna Cavalieri. When he was baptized, he receive the name (or names) Alfonso Maria Antonio Giovanni Cosmos Damien Michael Gaspard de Liguori, but he is known by the Latin form of his first name. He received the best education available to the noble class of Italians, an education that included painting, poetry, music (he played the harpsichord), dancing and fencing in addition to more serious subjects. He was also taught religious subjects by his devout mother and was taken on an annual retreat by his father, a stern disciplinarian who made sure that his children didn't waste their time.

Alphonsus certainly did not waste his time since he received a degree of doctor in both canon and civil law when he was only sixteen, and he was admitted to the bar when he was nineteen. For the next eight years he gained a reputation as an excellent lawyer, which greatly pleased his father. Alphonsus displeased his father, though, by twice avoiding what Don Joseph thought would be excellent marriages for his son.

Alphonsus's life changed when he lost a case

in court. He was representing a Neapolitan noble-man against a wealthy landowner from Tuscany and he was convinced of the justice of his side. Although he made a brilliant speech, he over-looked a small point of evidence, and he lost. It was a humiliating defeat, and Alphonsus eventu-ally came to think of it as God's way of telling him he wasn't supposed to be a lawyer. Although he had already been doing charitable work, he now spent more time visiting the sick while he prayed to learn what God's will for him was.

One day, while helping to care for the sick in the Hospital of the Incurables, Alphonsus saw a bright light and heard a voice saying, "Leave the world and give yourself to me." The same thing happened as he left the hospital. He went to the Church of Our Lady of Ransom where it occurred a third time. He took off his sword and belt, sym-bols of his nobility, and laid them on the Blessed Virgin's altar. He renounced his title and rights as the eldest son, and began to study for the priest-hood, to his father's great displeasure.

Even before his ordination, Alphonsus joined a group of priests who gave missions, acting as catechist for the priests. After ordination as a dea-con, he began preaching in the churches of Naples and it wasn't long before his fame as a preacher spread widely. He was ordained a priest on De-cember 21, 1726, when he was thirty, and began to devote himself full time to preaching and hearing confessions as part of a group of priests known as the Congregation of Apostolic Missions. Three years later he accepted an offer to be chaplain at the Chinese College, a seminary for prospective missionaries to China.

It was there that he met Father Thomas Falcoia, who became his spiritual director. Father Falcoia told Alphonsus about his vision concerning the founding of a religious Order of priests who would preach to the abandoned people. Alphonsus also met a nun, Sister Maria Celeste, who had similar visions. In 1730, after Father Falcoia had been made bishop of Castellamare, he asked Alphonsus to preach a retreat at Sister Maria Celeste's convent. While doing so, he examined the nun's visions and was convinced they were genuine. He revised the Rule which she had received in her visions and witnessed the establishment of the Redemptoristine Order on August 6, 1731.

Shortly after that, Sister Maria Celeste told Alphonsus that she had had other visions during which Christ ordered her to tell Alphonsus that he was to found a religious Order of priests and brothers who would preach to the abandoned country folk of the Kingdom of Naples. Alphonsus felt that he was already committed to the group of priests to which he belonged, but he went to Bishop Falcoia for advice. The bishop was enthusiastic about the idea so Alphonsus went about organizing a new institute. It was officially founded on

November 9, 1732 and was originally called the Congregation of the Most Holy Savior. However, there was already a religious order with a similar name. Therefore, when the institute received papal approbation in 1749, the name was changed to the Congregation of the Most Holy Redeemer. Its members are commonly known as Redemptorists.

Alphonsus began with seven companions, but the first year of the congregation was anything but peaceful. There was disagreement between Bishop Falcoia and Sister Maria Celeste over the Rule for the Order, and each member of the new Order had his own ideas about how the religious life should be lived. Alphonsus followed Bishop Falcoia, but he turned out to be alone in this allegiance. The disagreements became so bad that Sister Maria Celeste was expelled from her Order and all of Alphonsus's original companions, except for one lay brother, left to form another religious group.

But the Order survived as new postulants began to arrive — men who gladly accepted the Rule drawn up by Alphonsus. The Order soon established four other foundations, all in the mountains southeast of Naples. Pope Benedict XIV approved the Rule of the Redemptorists in 1749 and of the Redemptoristines in 1750.

Despite the furor in his Order, Alphonsus was devoting most of his time during the twenty-six years from 1726 to 1752 to the preaching of mis-

sions, traveling from one parish to another throughout the Kingdom of Naples. In 1752, when he was
fifty-six, various bodily ailments required him to
slow down a bit on the missions, but he continued the writing he had always done. Of one hundred ten books and pamphlets that he wrote, sixty-
four can be classified as ascetical or religious, thirty-
one as moral theology, and fifteen as dogmatic
theology. Many of these works are still being published today by Liguori Publications in Liguori,
Missouri. Among the most popular are *Glories of
Mary, Visits to the Blessed Sacrament and to the
Blessed Virgin, The True Spouse of Jesus Christ,* and
The Great Means of Prayer.

Alphonsus's style in his writing was similar
to the prayerful meditation he practiced and taught
to others. It consisted of a brief consideration of
some aspect of the mysteries of our redemption
followed by a prayer filled with feelings of love,
contrition and other sentiments of devotion. His
favorite devotions were to the Eucharist, to Christ
in his Passion, and to the Blessed Mother.

In 1747 Alphonsus was asked to become
archbishop of Palermo in Sicily, but he managed
to beg off from that assignment. But in 1762, Pope
Clement XIII ordered him to become bishop of
Saint Agatha of the Goths, a small diocese north-
east of Naples. In obedience, he went to Rome for
his consecration, the only time in his life that he
left the Kingdom of Naples.

He found a diocese badly in need of spiritual reform: more than thirty thousand uninstructed men and women and four hundred indifferent priests. He immediately had missions preached in every parish, making his own visitations to the parishes short missions. He reorganized the seminary and religious houses, taught theology, and wrote. During a severe famine in 1764, he sold practically all of his episcopal furniture to feed the poor. He did all this while continuing to serve as superior general of the Redemptorists and while suffering from the severe rheumatism that was beginning to deform his body.

In 1768, when he was seventy-one, Alphonsus's ailments became more severe. He suffered a bad attack of rheumatic fever that kept him in bed for more than a year. The illness left him partially paralyzed and the paralysis particularly affected his neck. He could not raise his head and the pressure of his chin caused an open wound on his chest. He had to drink through a tube. When saying Mass, while seated in a chair, the chair had to be tilted back so he could drink the Precious Blood.

Now he began to have mystical experiences. On September 21, 1774, he went into a seemingly lifeless trance that continued for a full day. When he came out of it, he calmly told those at his bedside, "I have been assisting the pope, who has just died." Later, word arrived that Pope Clement XIV had died on the morning of September 22.

Alphonsus tried repeatedly to resign as bishop of Saint Agatha of the Goths, pleading incapacitation, but his pleas went unheeded until 1775, when he was seventy-eight. He then moved to the Redemptorist headquarters in Pagani, thinking that he was preparing for death. But his trials were not over yet.

This was a time in history when the Society of Jesus was being suppressed in various European countries, and finally by Pope Clement XIV for the entire world. Now the Kingdom of Naples was looking askance at the Redemptorists, considering them nothing but Jesuits in disguise. To keep the Redemptorists from being suppressed, the vicar general of the Order, Father Villani, agreed in 1779 to a revised form of their Rule, which established them as secular priests. Alphonsus was then eighty-three, crippled, deaf, and nearly blind. Thinking he was doing the right thing, he signed the document presented by his vicar general. When he received the document, the pope declared all the members of the congregation in the Kingdom of Naples, including Alphonsus, to be no longer Redemptorists. Alphonsus was crushed when he learned that he had been betrayed, but he accepted the pope's decision. He died outside the religious Order he founded. It was not until 1793 that peace and unity were restored to the Redemptorists and they were allowed to continue their mission which eventually expanded to the whole world.

His death came on August 1, 1787, in his ninety-second year. He was beatified by Pope Pius VII in 1816, canonized by Pope Gregory XVI in 1839, declared a Doctor of the Church by Pope Pius IX in 1871, and named the patron of moral theologians and all priests engaged in hearing confessions by Pope Pius XII in 1953. The Church celebrates his feast on August 1.

From *Visits to the Most Blessed Sacrament and the Blessed Virgin Mary*, by Saint Alphonsus de Liguori

THIRD VISIT

"I am delighted to be with humanity." These are the words of our God. Dying for us was not enough for him. He wanted to remain with us in this Blessed Sacrament. "O men," moans Saint Teresa, "how can you offend a God who says that he is delighted to be with you?" He is highly pleased to be with us. Should we not find comfort and peace in being with him? Let us thank him for loving us and talk to him heart to heart.

Here I am, Lord, kneeling before this altar where you remain a "shut-in" for me night and day. You are the Fountain of grace, the Healer of the sick, the Helper of the helpless. Have mercy on a sick and helpless sinner. But I will not let my sad condition discourage me because I know that you are in this living bread to help me. I adore you! I thank you! I love you! Please listen as I plead with you: Give me the courage and the strength to love you.

Lord, I love you from the depths of my soul. I love you with all the love I own. Help me to put meaning into those words. Mary, my Mother, my patron saints, angels in heaven, help me to love my God.

Spiritual Communion: My Jesus, I believe you are really here in the Blessed Sacrament. I love you more than anything in the world, and I hunger to feed on your flesh. But since I cannot receive Communion at this moment, feed my soul at least spiritually. I unite myself to you as I do when I actually receive you. Never let me drift away from you.

Visit With Mary: "Her chains are saving chains." A certain holy man said that devotion to Mary is like a chain that pulls us up to heaven. Let us ask our Lady to keep drawing us to herself by that chain of trust and love, O kind, O loving, O sweet Virgin Mary!

Most Holy Immaculate Virgin and my Mother Mary, to you who are the Mother of my Lord, the Queen of the world, the Advocate, the Hope, the Refuge of sinners, I have recourse today — I, who am the most miserable of all. I render you my most humble homage, O great Queen, and I thank you for all the graces you have conferred on me until now, particularly for having delivered me from hell, which I have so often deserved. I love you, O most amiable Lady; and for the love which I bear you, I promise to serve you always and to do all in my power to make others also love you. I place in you all my hopes; I confide my salvation to your care. Accept me for your servant and receive me under your mantle, O Mother of Mercy. And since you are so powerful with God, deliver me from all temptations, or rather obtain for me the strength to triumph over them until death. Of you I ask a perfect love for Jesus Christ. From you I hope to die a good death. O my Mother, by the love which you bear to God, I beseech you to help me at all times, but especially at the last moment of my life. Leave me not, I beseech you, until you see me safe in heaven, blessing you and singing your mercies for all eternity.

Amen. So I hope. So may it be.

From *The Glories of Mary,* by Saint Alphonsus

To you do we send up our sighs, mourning and weeping in this valley of tears.

It is an article of faith that it is not only allowable but useful to invoke the saints, and especially the Queen of Saints, that they may obtain grace for us. This doctrine was defined by general councils against heretics who said that such a teaching was injurious to Jesus Christ, our only Mediator. In addition, Jeremiah prayed for Jerusalem after his death, the ancients of the Book of Revelation presented the prayers of the saints to God, Saint Peter promised his disciples that after his death he would be mindful of them. And Saint Stephen prayed for his persecutors, and Saint Paul for his companions.

Hence, if the saints can themselves pray for us, why can we not beseech them to pray for us? Indeed, Saint Paul commended himself to the prayers of his disciples and Saint James exhorts us to pray for one another. Then we can do the same....

No one denies that Jesus Christ is our only Mediator of justice. By his merits he has won our reconciliation with God. But, on the other hand, it is impious to maintain that God is not pleased to grant graces at the intercession of his saints — and particularly of Mary his mother, whom Jesus desires so much to see loved and honored by all....

Who will pretend that the honor bestowed on a mother does not redound to the honor of her son? So Saint Bernard says, "Let us not imagine that we obscure the glory of the Son by the great praise we lavish on the mother; for the more she is honored, the greater is the glory of her Son. There can be no doubt that whatever we say in praise of the mother gives equal praise to the Son."

By the merits of Jesus, Mary was made the mediatrix of our salvation; not a mediatrix of justice, of course, but of grace and intercession — as Saint Bonaventure expressly calls her: "Mary, the most faithful mediatrix of our salvation."…

What we intend to prove here is that Mary's intercession is not only useful, but necessary for salvation: not absolutely, but morally, necessary. This necessity goes back to the very will of God himself, who had decreed that all the graces he gives human beings should pass through Mary's hands. This is the opinion of Saint Bernard — an opinion which we may now safely call the general opinion of theologians and Doctors.

Mediation of justice by way of merit (and this is Christ's mediation) is one thing, and mediation of grace by way of prayer (our Lady's mediation) is another. Besides, it is one thing to say that God cannot, and another that he *will* not, give graces without the intercession of Mary.

From *The Passion and Death of Jesus Christ,* by Saint Alphonsus

Jesus Christ could easily have obtained for us salvation without suffering, and in leading a life of ease and delight: but no, Saint Paul says, "Having joy set before him, he endured the cross." He refused the riches, the delights, the honors of the world, and chose for himself a life of poverty, and death full of suffering and ignominy. And wherefore? Would it not have sufficed for him to have offered to his eternal Father one single prayer for the pardon of man? For this prayer, being of infinite value, would have been sufficient to save the world, and infinite worlds besides. Why, then, did he choose for himself so much suffering, and a death so cruel, that an author has said very truly, that through mere pain the soul of Jesus separated itself from his body?

Saint John Chrysostom answers, a single prayer of Jesus would have indeed sufficed to redeem us; but it was not sufficient to show us the love that our God has borne us: "That which sufficed to redeem us was not sufficient for love."

And Saint Thomas confirms this when he says, "Christ, in suffering from love, offered to God more than the expiation demanded by the offense of the human race." Because Jesus loved us so much, he desired to be loved very much by us; and therefore he did everything he could, even unto suffering for us, in order to conciliate our love, and to show that there was nothing more that he could do to make us love him: "He endured much weariness," says Saint Bernard, "that he might bind man to love him much."

And what greater proof of love, says our Savior himself, can a friend show towards the person he loves than to give his life for his sake?

"Greater love than this no man has, that a man lay down his life for his friends."

But you, O most loving Jesus, says Saint Bernard, have done more than this, since you have given your life for us, who were not your friends, but your enemies, and rebels against you: "You have a greater charity, Lord, in giving your life for your enemies." ...

You would then die for me, your enemy, O my Jesus, and yet can I resist so much love? Behold, here I am; since you do anxiously desire that I should love you, I will drive away every other love from my breast, and will love you alone.

Chapter 33

SAINT THÉRÈSE OF LISIEUX

Saint Thérèse of Lisieux is undoubtedly one of the most popular of all the saints. More people have a devotion to her than to any of the other Doctors of the Church, perhaps even to any other saint except the Blessed Virgin. One seldom hears of people praying to Saint Thomas Aquinas, Saint Augustine, or Saint Albert the Great, but many people pray frequently to Saint Thérèse — more than to any of the other Doctors with the possible exception of Saint Anthony of Padua for those who lose things frequently. She is widely known as "the Little Flower."

Yet Thérèse might seem to be an unlikely Doctor. She was not learned, did not perform any great deeds, and was almost completely unknown during her lifetime. She lived in obscurity in a cloistered convent in France, scarcely distinguished from the numerous other nuns who live similar lives. In fact, before she died Thérèse overheard two other nuns discussing the obituary that would be written and sent to other Carmelite convents after she died. They wondered what could be written in hers that would be of interest since she had never done anything exceptional.

Nevertheless, by her life she taught us how to live. She showed us that the way to perfection lies in performing the small daily things well and putting up with suffering and aggravations pleasantly — what she called her "Little Way." Perhaps that is enough to be declared one of the thirty-three greatest teachers in the history of the Church. At least that's what Pope John Paul II thought when he proclaimed her a Doctor of the Church on the hundredth anniversary of her death in 1997, the third woman to receive this honor.

Most of what we know about Thérèse comes from her autobiography, *L'histoire d'un Âme* (*The Story of a Soul*), which she wrote during the last two years of her life.

Marie Françoise Thérèse was born on January 2, 1873 in Alençon, France to Louis Martin, a watchmaker, and Zelie-Marie Guérin, a maker of the famous Alençon lace. The Martins had nine children, but two boys and two girls died in infancy; five daughters lived to maturity. Thérèse was the youngest. All five of the girls were to become nuns.

Her childhood was apparently normal, and happy. She wrote that her first memories were of smiles and caresses. Her parents went to daily Mass and the family gathered for prayers each evening.

It wasn't long, though, before sadness entered her life: Her mother died when she was only four. Her father then gave up his business and moved his family to Lisieux, in Normandy, where Madame Martin's brother lived with his wife and family. The Martin children were put under the watchful eye of Madame Guérin, but it was Thérèse's oldest sister Marie, then seventeen, who ran the household. Another sister, sixteen-year-old Pauline, gave religious instructions to her younger sisters: fourteen-year-old Leonie, eight-year-old Céline, and Thérèse. Pauline was the greatest influence on Thérèse as she grew up.

Pauline was also the first of the girls to leave home — to enter the Carmelite convent across town — when she was twenty-one and Thérèse nine. Pauline's decision enkindled in Thérèse her own desire for religious life, a desire that was intensified four years later when Marie followed Pauline. During this time she was receiving her education from the Benedictine nuns of the Notre-Dame-du-Pre convent.

On Christmas Eve of 1886, ten days before her fourteenth birthday, Thérèse had a mystical experience that she later called "my conversion." It was to affect the rest of her life. She described it this way: "On that blessed night the sweet infant Jesus, scarcely an hour old, filled the darkness of my soul with floods of light. By becoming weak and little, for love of me, he made me strong and brave: He put his own weapons into my hands so that I went on from strength to strength, beginning, if I may say so, 'to run as a giant.'" It was because of this vision of Jesus as a child that she later chose as her name in religious life Thérèse of the Child Jesus.

Thérèse told her father that she wanted to join her sisters in the Carmelite convent, and her father readily consented. The Carmelites, though, thought that she was too young. When the Martins went to the bishop, he agreed to think about it. A few months later, Louis Martin took Thérèse and Céline on a pilgrimage to Rome as part of the Jubilee Year proclaimed by Pope Leo XIII — the only time Thérèse was to leave France during her entire life. The pilgrimage included an audience with the pope.

In a letter from Rome to her sister Pauline, now known as Sister Agnès of Jesus, Thérèse described what happened next: "The pope was sitting on a great chair; M. Reverony was near him; he watched the pilgrims kiss the pope's foot and pass before him and spoke a word about some of them. Imagine how my heart beat as I saw my turn come: I didn't want to return without speaking to the pope. I spoke, but I did not get it all said because M. Reverony did not give me time. He said immediately: 'Most Holy Father, she is a child who wants to enter Carmel at fifteen, but its superiors are considering the matter at the moment.' I would have liked to be able to explain my case, but there was no way. The Holy Father said to me simply: 'If the good God wills, you will enter.' Then I was made to pass on to another room. Pauline, I cannot tell you what I felt. It was like annihilation, I felt deserted.... Still God cannot be giving me trials beyond my strength. He gave me the courage to sustain this one."

Despite Thérèse's feeling of "annihilation," the bishop finally decided to allow her to join the convent and the Carmelites admitted her in the Carmel at Lisieux on April 9, 1888. She was fifteen. She was immensely happy and her happiness was contagious among the other Sisters. She loved the daily routine of liturgical prayers and the reading of Scripture. This was where she spent the rest of her short life.

The year after Thérèse entered the Carmel, her father suffered two paralyzing strokes followed by a mental breakdown. He had to be put in a private sanitarium where he remained for three years. Thérèse calmly accepted this calamity, writing, "The three years of my father's martyrdom seem to me the dearest and most fruitful of our life. I would not exchange them for the most sublime ecstasies."

She took her final vows on September 8, 1890 when she was seventeen. Even with poor health, she carried out all the austerities of the Carmelite order, with one exception: she was not permitted to fast. The hardship that she felt more than any other, she confessed on her deathbed, was the cold of the convent buildings during the winter. However, she never complained about it.

When she was twenty she was appointed to assist the novice mistress, and was novice mistress in all but name.

Louis Martin died in 1894 when Thérèse was twenty-one and soon thereafter Céline, who had been caring for him, became the fourth sister from the Martin family to enter the Carmel at Lisieux. Some years later, Leonie joined a different Order, that of the Visitation Sisters.

Thérèse had long been aware that her vocation as a Carmelite was to love, and her love for God and for others continued to grow. It was not always easy. She once wrote in her autobiography that she was bothered during meditation by one of the other Sisters who was constantly fidgeting with her rosary. Therefore, she wrote, "Instead of trying not to hear it, which was impossible, I set myself to listen as though it had been some delightful music, and my meditation, which was *not* the 'prayer of quiet,' passed in offering this music to our Lord."

No one knew more about Thérèse than her sister Pauline, who by now was the Carmel's prioress and known as Mother Agnès of Jesus. It was she who told Thérèse to write *Story of a Soul*, although the idea first came to Thérèse's oldest sister, Marie. As the three sisters were reminiscing one evening in the convent, and Thérèse recalled some of the things that happened after their mother died, Marie suggested that she put some of her recollections in writing. When Thérèse laughed at the idea, Marie asked Pauline, as prioress, to put Thérèse under obedience. She did. On the cover of each of the manuscripts that made up the book, Thérèse wrote, "Notebook of Obedience." The title *L'histoire d'un Âme* or *The Story of a Soul* was given to the book when it was published a year after her death.

The Story of a Soul is actually three manuscripts. Manuscript A is the one asked for by Mother Agnès (Pauline), Thérèse's memory of her life before entering the convent. Manuscript B tells us about Thérèse's "Little Way," for which she is famous. Thérèse wrote it as a letter to Marie after Marie asked her to explain the "Little Way." Manuscript C is Thérèse's memoirs of her experience as a Carmelite, and she wrote it in obedience to Mother Gonzague, who succeeded Mother Agnès as prioress, at the suggestion of Mother Agnès.

Thérèse also wrote many letters, sometimes to missionaries. She wrote to Carmelite sisters in Hanoi, and to Père Roulland, a missionary in China. She also exchanged twenty-one letters with a seminarian, Maurice Belliere, after he wrote to the Carmel asking to have a nun assigned to pray for him. She continued this correspondence until her death.

When Thérèse was twenty-three she contracted tuberculosis, a disease for which there was no cure. Her lungs hemorrhaged for the first time on Good Friday of 1896. At the same time, she began to experience a period of spiritual darkness, what Saint John of the Cross called "the dark night of the soul." It was a trial that she endured for the rest of her brief life. She described that darkness in her autobiography.

Thérèse lived with tuberculosis for eighteen months, during which time she suffered terribly. She died on September 30, 1897 with the words, "My God, I love thee!" on her lips after she sat up in her bed and was gazing at a space above a statue of the Blessed Virgin. She obviously had had a vision.

After the book *The Story of a Soul* was published a year later, Thérèse quickly became one of the most beloved saints of all time. Her story reached around the world. Dorothy Day was converted by reading her autobiography and later wrote her own biography of Thérèse. Thomas Merton, Graham Greene, Georges Bernanos, Teilhard de Chardin, Hans Urs von Balthasar, and Jean Guitton were only a few who were influenced by her. Mother Teresa of Calcutta took her name, not from Saint Teresa of Avila, but from Saint Thérèse of Lisieux.

Pope Pius XI beatified Thérèse in 1923, only twenty-six years after her death. Two years later, in 1925, he canonized her. In 1927 he named her patroness of foreign missions along with Saint Francis Xavier. Pope John Paul II declared her a Doctor of the Church in 1997. The Church celebrates her feast on October 1.

From *The Story of a Soul,*
by Saint Thérèse of the Child Jesus

Since my longing for martyrdom was powerful and unsettling, I turned to the epistles of Saint Paul in the hope of finally finding an answer. By chance the twelfth and thirteenth chapters of the First Epistle to the Corinthians caught my attention, and in the first section I read that not everyone can be an apostle, prophet or teacher, that the Church is composed of a variety of members, and that the eye cannot be the hand. Even with such an answer revealed before me, I was not satisfied and did not find peace.

I persevered in the reading and did not let my mind wander until I found this encouraging theme: "Set your desires on the greater gifts. And I will now show you the way which surpasses all others." For the Apostle insists that the greater gifts are nothing at all without love and that this same love is surely the best path leading directly to God. At length I had found peace of mind.

When I had looked upon the Mystical Body of the Church, I recognized myself in none of the members which Saint Paul described, and what is more, I desired to distinguish myself more favorably within the whole body. Love appeared to me to be the hinge for my vocation. Indeed I knew that the Church had a body composed of various members, but in this body the necessary and more noble member was not lacking; I knew that the Church had a heart and that such a heart appeared to be aflame with love. I knew that one love drove the members of the Church to action, that if this love were extinguished, the apostles would have proclaimed the Gospel no longer, the martyrs would have shed their blood no more. I saw and realized that love sets off the bounds of all vocations, that love is everything, that this same love embraces every time and every place. In one word, that love is everlasting.

Then, nearly ecstatic with the supreme joy of my soul, I proclaimed: O Jesus, my love, at last I have found my calling: my call is love. Certainly I have found my proper place in the Church, and you gave me that very place, my God. In the heart of the Church, my mother, I will be love, and thus I will be all things, as my desire finds its direction.

From a Letter to Her Sister Marie, by Saint Thérèse

Let me tell you, Marie, that my desires for martyrdom are *nothing*. It is not they which give me the unlimited confidence which I feel in my heart. What pleases God in my little soul is *that he sees me loving my littleness and my poverty: it is the blind hope that I have in his mercy.* That is my only treasure. Why can it not be yours? …

To love Jesus, the more one is weak, without desires and without virtues, the more one is suitable for the operations of consuming and transforming love. It is confidence and nothing but confidence that must lead us to love.

Saint Thérèse Describes Her Night of Nothingness, from *The Story of a Soul*

[Jesus] allowed my soul to be overrun by an impenetrable darkness, which made the thought of heaven, hitherto so welcome, a subject of nothing but conflict and torment.

I try to refresh my jaded spirits with the thought of that bright country where my hopes lie; and what happens? It is worse torment than ever; the darkness itself seems to borrow from the sinners who live in it the gift of speech. I hear its mocking accents: "It's all a dream, this talk of heaven bathed in light, and of a God who made it all, who is to be your possession in eternity! You really believe, do you, that the mist which hangs about you will clear away later on? All right, go on longing for death. But death will make nonsense of your hopes; it will only mean a night darker than ever, the night of mere nonexistence."...

I don't suppose I've made as many acts of faith in all the rest of my life as I have during this past year. Every time the conflict is renewed, at each challenge from the enemy, I give a good account of myself — by meeting him face to face? Oh no, only a coward accepts the challenge to a duel. No, I turn my back in contempt, and take refuge in Jesus, telling him that I'm ready to defend the doctrine of heaven with the last drop of my blood. What does it matter, that I should catch no glimpse of its beauties, here on earth, if that will help poor sinners to see them in eternity?

Short Reflections from *The Story of a Soul,* by Saint Thérèse

I will spend my heaven doing good on earth.

I have never given the good God aught but love, and it is with love that he will repay.

My "little way" is the way of spiritual childhood; the way of trust and absolute self-surrender.

I am a very little soul, who can offer only very little things to the Lord.

Above all it's the Gospels that occupy my mind when I'm at prayer; my poor soul has so many needs, and yet this is the one thing needful. I'm always finding fresh lights there, hidden and enthralling meanings.

From the Last Letter from Saint Thérèse to Maurice Belliere

August 10, 1897

My dear little Brother,

I am now all ready to leave. I have my passport for heaven, and it is my dear Father who has obtained this grace for me. On the 19th he gave me the assurance that I would soon go to join him. The next day the doctor, astonished by the progress the sickness had made in two days, said to Mother that it was time to grant my wish to receive Extreme Unction. So I had this happiness on the 30th, and also that of seeing Jesus in the Blessed Sacrament leave the tabernacle and come to me, whom I received as viaticum for my long voyage! This Bread of Heaven has strengthened me. Just look, it seems as if my pilgrimage can't get to its destination. Far from complaining about this, I rejoice that God still lets me suffer for love of him.

Ah, how good it is to let yourself go in his arms, with neither fears nor desires.

I have to tell you, little brother, that we don't understand heaven in the same way. You think that, once I share in the justice and holiness of God, I won't be able to excuse your faults as I did when I was on earth. Are you then forgetting that I shall also share in the *infinite mercy* of the Lord? I believe that the Blessed in heaven have great compassion for our miseries. They remember that when they were weak and mortal like us, they committed the same faults themselves and went through the same struggles, and their fraternal tenderness becomes still greater than it ever was on earth. It's on account of this that they never stop watching over us and praying for us.

Now my dear little brother, I must tell you about the *inheritance you* will come into after my death. Here is the share which our Mother will give you: (1) the reliquary which I received on the day I took the habit and which has never left me since then; (2) a little crucifix which is incomparably more dear to me than the large one, for the one I have now is no longer the first one that I was given. In Carmel we sometimes exchange holy objects; it is a way of keeping us from getting attached to them.

Let me come back to the little crucifix. It is not beautiful; the face of Christ has disappeared. You won't be surprised at this when I tell you that since I was 13 years old this souvenir from one of my sisters has followed me everywhere. It was especially during my voyage in Italy that the crucifix became dear to me. I touched it to all the famous relics I had the joy of venerating, which were more than I can count, and moreover it was blessed by the Holy Father. Ever since I've been sick, I hold our dear little crucifix almost constantly in my hands, and as I look at it now I think with joy that after having received my kisses it will go to claim those of my little brother. Look then what a *heritage* you will have! In addition, our Mother will give you the last picture that I painted.

A Dieu, dear little brother, may God give us the grace to love him and to save souls for him. This is the wish of

Your unworthy little Sister of the Child Jesus
and of the Holy Face

SOURCES FOR EXCERPTS FROM WRITINGS OF
DOCTORS OF THE CHURCH
Volume Two

Saint Peter Damian: From the Life of Saint Romuald, June 19; From a Letter, February 21; From a Sermon on Feast of St. George, April 23

Saint Anselm: Excerpts from the *Proslogion*, Friday of First Week of Advent and April 21

Saint Bernard: From a Sermon on the Song of Songs, Wednesday of Third Week; From a Homily in Praise of the Virgin Mother, Tuesday of Twentieth Week; From a Sermon on Guardian Angels, October 2

Saint Albert the Great: From Commentary on the Gospel of Luke: November 15

Saint Thomas Aquinas: Lecture on Feast of Corpus Christi

Saint Bonaventure: Discourse on the Sacred Heart: Feast of the Sacred Heart

Saint Catherine of Siena: Two excerpts from *The Dialogue*: April 29 and Saturday of Thirty-First Week

St. Teresa of Avila: Prayer by Saint Teresa: Compline for Wednesdays; From *The Way of Perfection*, Wednesday of Thirteenth Week; From a work by Saint Teresa, October 15 (her feast)

St. John of the Cross: From *The Spiritual Canticle*, December 14 (his feast)

St. Peter Canisius: From *Testament*, December 21 (his feast)

St. Robert Bellarmine: From *On the Ascent of the Mind to God:* September 19 (his feast)

St. Lawrence of Brindisi: From a sermon: July 21 (his feast)

St. Francis de Sales: From *The Introduction to the Devout Life,* January 24 (his feast)

St. Thérèse of the Child Jesus: From *The Story of a Soul:* October 1 (her feast)

From *Lives of Saints,* copyright 1954 and 1963 by John J. Crawley & Co.:

Saint Anthony of Padua: From *Sermons for the Liturgical Year.* Acknowledgment given to *Les Sermons de St. Antoine de Padoue pour l'année Liturgique,* translated by Abbé Paul Bayart. Paris, n.d., prior to 1953.

Saint Albert the Great: Decretal Letter of Canonization, by Pope Pius XI, 1931.

Saint Teresa of Avila: Excerpts from *The Interior Castle,* London, 1912.

Saint John of the Cross: Second excerpt from *The Ascent of Mount Carmel:* From *The Complete Works of Saint John of the Cross,* translated by E. Allison Peers, published by Burns & Oates Ltd., 1935 and 1953.

Saint Peter Canisius: Letter to Cardinal John Morone: From Biblioteca Apostolica Vaticana, Vatican City.

Saint Alphonsus Liguori: From *The Passion and Death of Jesus Christ:* Redemptorist Fathers, *The Complete Works of Alphonsus de Liguori (The Ascetical Works).*

From *Saint of the Day* (St. Anthony Messenger Press)

Saint Lawrence of Brindisi: From a Sermon

Random House

Saint Thomas Aquinas: Excerpts from *Summa Theologiae* from *Basic Writings of Saint Thomas Aquinas,* copyright 1945.

B. Herder Book Co.

Saint Bonaventure: Excerpt from *Psalter of Our Lady*, translated by Paul M. Byrne, L.S.M.

E. P. Dutton & Co.

Saint Catherine of Siena: From Letter to Pope Gregory XI: *Letters of St. Catherine of Siena,* translated by Vida D. Scudder in 1906.

Paulist Press

Saint John of the Cross: Excerpts from *The Ascent of Mount Carmel* and *The Dark Night*: From *John of the Cross; Selected Writings,* edited by Kieran Kavanaugh, O.C.D., copyright 1987 by the Washington Province of Discalced Carmelite Friars, Inc., and published by Paulist Press as one of its "Classics of Western Spirituality."

Image Books (Doubleday)

Saint Francis de Sales: Three excerpts from *Introduction to the Devout Life*. Translated and edited by John K. Ryan, copyright 1966. Originally published in 1966 by Harper & Row.

Liguori Publications

St. Alphonsus Liguori: From *Visits to the Most Blessed Sacrament and the Blessed Virgin Mary.*

Catholic Book Publishing Co.

St. Alphonsus Liguori: From *The Glories of Mary.*

Doubleday